For Jessica, with love.

I Watched Football Early the Day I Died:

The Lost Ed Wood Frank Leahy Screenplay

by

W. Paul Apel

with

Greg Javer and Bob Blackburn

The Frank Leahy Legend

screenplay by Edward D. Wood, Jr. based on the book of the same name by Bernie J. Williams, edited and reissued by K. Raven Rozier as

Iron Desire: The Legacy of Notre Dame Football Coach Frank Leahy

BearManor Media.com

I Watched Football Early the Day I Died: The Lost Ed Wood Frank Leahy Screenplay

Typesetting and layout by PKJ Passion Global

Cover art by Patrick Truby

Published in the USA by
BearManor Media
1317 Edgewater Dr #110
Orlando FL 32804
www.BearManorMedia.com

Softcover Edition
ISBN-10:
ISBN-13: 979-8-88771-211-6

Published in the USA by Bear Manor Media

Foreword

"Poor Eddie... my darling Eddie."

This was how Ed Wood Jr.'s widow and my friend Kathleen O'Hara Wood would occasionally start our regular afternoon chats when I got home to our apartment building in the heart of Hollywood. I had moved there from Seattle in March of 1989 to work in radio. I picked the five-story building near the corner of Franklin and Cahuenga because it was only six blocks or so from where I was going to be working as a "board operator" at KIIS-FM. It was an old funky building with a mix of young folks trying to break into the film and TV business, older retired folks living on their Social Security pensions, a few drug dealers and, believe it or not, a transvestite hooker or two. The surrounding neighborhood, a few blocks from the heart of the area's famed Hollywood Blvd., was controlled by the 18th Street Gang. There were gunshots on weekend nights and graffiti was all over the place, but it was cheap and close to work.

I used to run into an elderly lady walking her very old dog now and then and knew she lived in the building. I'm a friendly guy, so I would always say hello and how are you. Once in a while I would walk with her down to the bus stop, she on her way to go shopping and I on the way to my second radio job.

Through a weird set of circumstances I attended an "Ed-Wood-A-Thon" film festival in 1992, my first immersion into the world of cult film director Edward D. Wood, Jr. While watching a documentary about Ed that had been made a few years earlier I saw a lady interviewed talking about her late husband. The film identified her as Kathy Wood – Ed Wood's widow. She looked very familiar so when I got home from the film festival I checked the mailbox in the lobby for the lady I saw walking her dog all the time, and it said "K. Wood". Thus began my still continuing journey in the wild and wacky world of Edward D. Wood, Jr.

I became friends with Kathy when I helped her get an entertainment lawyer to help her deal with Disney film studios when the 1994 Johnny Depp/Tim Burton film *Ed Wood* was in production. She was in her early 70s. I would take her grocery shopping and we'd even go see a movie from time to time. Her love of movies was one of the things that had originally attracted her to Ed Wood. Since

I have no immediate family in L.A. and no romantic entanglements, I would usually go down and visit with her for an hour or two in the late afternoon, early evening after I got home from my radio job. It was then that Kathy would start talking, sometimes about herself, but mainly about her beloved "Eddie".

She talked about their life together from mid 1956 when they first met and Ed was on the rebound after his failed marriage to Norma McCarty, which ended abruptly when she discovered that Ed was a cross dresser, to Ed's tragic passing from a heart attack only three days after their eviction from their Yucca St. apartment which was just over the back fence from where our building was. She knew the neighborhood, and still had a few friends in it, which was why she chose to move back nearby after his death. She talked about their life together, how they met, fell in love, got married, about Ed's work in films, his dreams, their hopes, their ups but mainly their downs, the drinking, the arguments and the trying to stay one step ahead of the bill collectors and landlords until December 7th 1978 when time ran out and they were evicted from their hovel of an apartment where they were six months overdue on their rent.

The sheriffs came in and threw Ed, Kathy and their scant possessions out on the sidewalk. All they had left was a small suitcase, filled with some papers including a manuscript for a book Ed had been working on since 1965 called *Hollywood Rat Race* and the script for a film near and dear to his heart titled *I Woke Up Early the Day I Died.*

In all of our many conversations, Kathy never mentioned the projects that Ed was working on in his later days, in the early 1970s up until their eviction. She knew about some of what he did, like his writing for Bernie Bloom at Pendulum Publishing where Ed cranked out short stories, articles and copy for pictorials, and Ed's work on some of the "adult" films that Bernie and his associates were starting to distribute. Ed was an early pioneer in the pornography business, but he kept much of this hidden from Kathy.

During those years they didn't go out much, mainly watching old movies on TV with some of their friends. Ed would also show a copy of *Plan 9 From Outer Space* on a projector he had kept. But Kathy never said anything about Ed and sports, like baseball, tennis, golf, or football. I don't think Ed was much into sports as from what I can tell he didn't play them when he was young. During his teenage high school years he much preferred watching movies at the local Poughkeepsie, N.Y. Bardovan Theater where, much to his delight, he eventually got a job as an usher, getting to see all his favorite films and actors not only for free, but getting paid. He also collected lobby cards and posters. He was into radio back in the 1930s, then at its height, as well as comic books and adventure stories. There was no time for or interest in sports as far as can be discerned. Plus, who knows if he was already wearing girls' undergarments by then, which he certainly did for most of his adult life. If so, he wouldn't have been able to undress in an all male locker room. It was much better to wear such things under an usher's uniform.

Which is why the discovery of the script *The Frank Leahy Legend* comes as a shock. I wonder if Kathy ever knew about it? I would think she would have as it was a job for hire separate from Ed's other work at Pendulum or the occasional scripts he'd sell to Stephen Apostolof which were more in the "R" rated category of films. A job to create a script from a book already written and published based on a legendary Notre Dame football player and coach just sounds too wild on the surface, but during those dire times I am sure whatever work Ed could get he and Kathy were grateful for, even though in the long run time ran out. I will let Greg and Paul delve into the writing, the style and the things that make this such a "Woodian" endeavor. I just wanted to give a little background into the lives of Ed and Kathy Wood.

In the early 2000s, Kathy Wood prepared a statement about her life and time with Eddie to fight a probate case brought against her by Ed's first wife Norma McCarty, which was eventually thrown out by the judge. She ended this statement in the following way. I'll let her have the last word...

"...Beulah had just gone in to say hello. In a second she came out, and said 'Kathy, you had better come in….Eddie's gone.' Somehow I knew what she meant. He was lying there propped up in bed, eyes wide open in terror, just staring. I'll never forget that look.

Our world had ended.

Eddie died at 10:30 a.m. on Sunday Dec. 10th, 1978… Alone… watching a FOOTBALL game! Eddie hated football."

Bob Blackburn
Friend and neighbor of Kathy Wood, Ed Wood, Jr.'s widow
2022

Bob Blackburn and Kathy Wood.

When Legends Collide

By Greg Javer

"Show me a gracious loser, and I'll show you a failure."

– Knute Rockne

In post-revolutionary 1837 France, blessed Father Basil Moreau founded the Congregation of Holy Cross. Within a few years, he sent six Brothers – four of them of Irish descent – to the United States to extend the mission. In 1842, they established the University of Notre Dame du Lac, the first permanent foundation of the Congregation in the United States. Today, you'll recognize this cultural institution simply as Notre Dame.

A little over a hundred years later, in 1946, the Holy Cross Fathers extended their mission to Wilkes-Barre, Pennsylvania. They created King's College, a small liberal arts school I attended from 1986 through 1990. Many of my professors were priests, and they were a funny, smart, and encouraging bunch. I received a wonderful education there, and the curiosity they inspired in me then remains with me to this day. The school's connection to Notre Dame was never brought up, nor was football, as the school did not have a team (it does now, as King's College has grown over time).

I recognized just how important the legacy of Notre Dame football was to many people long before I attended King's. When there were only four channels on the television dial, it was hard to avoid college football games on a Saturday. Everyone drank the same Kool Aid. Notre Dame football was a sacred tradition; the program seemed to possess a magical *gravitas*.

Ara Parseghian was coaching the Irish in the early '70s when I was a wee lad. Little did I know back then about the storied lineage of Notre Dame football coaches – especially Knute Rockne (1888-1931), the coach to whom all others would be compared. Rockne's life was tragically cut short by a plane crash in March 1931, supposedly while on his way to participate in a film called *The Spirit of Notre Dame*. At the time of his death, the coach was at the zenith of his powers, having won back-to-back national championships in 1929 and 1930.

One of Rockne's tackles during his final three years as coach was a tenacious Nebraskan named Frank Leahy (1908-1973). After his playing days were over, Leahy served as a line coach at Georgetown, Michigan State, and Fordham before becoming head coach at Boston College. Finally, in 1941, he assumed the role of head coach at his beloved alma mater, later ludicrously claiming that "noder dame" were among the first words he ever spoke as a child. At Notre Dame, Leahy shepherded the team to four additional national championships while toiling in Knute Rockne's long shadow. Interestingly, the story of Frank Leahy intersects with that of Edward D. Wood, Jr., the man whose life and work I began strenuously researching about six years ago.

I'd never even heard the name Frank Leahy prior to seeing an undated screenplay called *The Frank Leahy Legend* listed in a résumé that Ed Wood supplied to budding filmmaker Fred Olen Ray in 1978. While the coach's name was unfamiliar to me, blogger Joe Blevins noted that Leahy was a Notre Dame football coach and that a book with that title had been released in 1974, the year after Leahy's passing. For years, I accepted this as just about all we would likely ever know. The project was not even mentioned in Rudolph Grey's *Nightmare of Ecstasy* (1992). The only additional information came from the résumé itself. Ed parenthetically noted "Scotty Williams Ent." alongside the listing, suggesting that the film got far enough along to attract a producer. Unfortunately, that name and production company drew blanks in my searching.

With no more leads to follow, I set Frank Leahy aside for a few years and focused on other aspects of the Wood story. But about a year ago, I was listening to a new episode of *These Days Are Ours: A Happy Days Podcast*, cohosted by Joe Blevins. Joe mentioned Leahy as one of the main candidates responsible for the famous sports quote, "When the going gets tough, the tough get going." This spurred me to do a little digging, and although I found little, a March 1975 article in the *Chicago Tribune* suggested that perhaps the film *almost* got made. Other than this one article – a mishmash of Chicagoland entertainment snippets by a local columnist – there is no evidence that it did. The article claims that a film titled *The Frank Leahy Legend* was slated to begin filming in Chicago that summer. Could this be Eddie's screenplay?

While that's plausible and seems to fit, there's no direct evidence that this movie would have been based on Eddie's script. Leahy passed in 1973, and the following year saw no fewer than three books devoted to his "legend." Published by JCL Services of Torrance, California, *The Frank Leahy Legend* is a collection of interviews with the coach conducted by one of his "closest friends," Bernard J. Williams. The book was republished in 2009 with modernized language as *Iron Desire: The Legacy of Notre Dame Football Coach Frank Leahy.*

Reading Williams' book today, it's hard to imagine what may have attracted Ed Wood to write about Frank Leahy in the first place. Was it simply an opportunity that presented itself? Did Eddie note that, in the immediate wake of Leahy's passing, a nostalgic interest and veritable (albeit tiny) cottage industry had grown up around Leahy? Or was he, unbeknownst to us all, a secret Notre Dame football fanatic?

As for Ed Wood's screenplay, Joe Blevins recently clued me into the fact that it apparently still survives, held in an archive at Loyola Marymount University and credited as 1975. The book itself is largely mythmaking on Leahy's part, while Williams' fawning wraparound text is never shy to remind us of Leahy's greatness. We're told how tough and persistent he was and how legendary he is. Frankly, the book is barely readable alpha-male claptrap, unless perhaps you are a dyed-in-the-wool Notre Dame football junkie. It's puzzling to me to understand this staunch allegiance, where Notre Dame football trumps even God, country and flag. Was this the original intent of the Holy Cross Fathers' Mission?

Finally, it's worth noting what is almost certainly a strange coincidence. The fabled "Four Horseman of the Apocalypse" – Notre Dame's legendary backfield—led the Fightin' Irish to their first National Championship in 1924. Among them was Don Miller. If that name rings a bell, yes, it was the pseudonym under which Ed Wood produced and directed the adult feature *Necromania* (1971). In a related note, Frank Leahy was utterly obsessed with the death of Knute Rockne and at times refused to believe his mentor was truly dead.

While these are just a few crumbs of information, they do give us something to chew on. A few things, really: Did *The Frank Leahy Legend*, based upon Eddie's script, make it to pre-production? Could it have gone into production? Is Eddie's script truly extant? Was

Eddie really a football fan? Did he look up to Leahy, whose warped "win at all costs" value system was so antithetical to how Ed lived his life?

Persistence is key, folks, as Frank Leahy often noted. And don't forget, it's a game of inches, and the vast majority of plays don't result in a touchdown.

From Williams to Wood: What (Little) We Know

by W. Paul Apel

Perhaps the most confounding entry on Ed Wood's résumé is the mysterious unproduced screenplay *The Frank Leahy Legend*, written for the equally mysterious Scotty Williams Entertainment, and based on a book of the same name by Bernard J. Williams.

I didn't even know it existed until I read about it in Greg Javer's article on Joe Blevins' blog, Ed Wood Wednesdays. Up until now, no Ed Wood experts have read the screenplay or reviewed it, let alone published their findings. It's not even mentioned in the seminal source of Ed Wood knowledge, Rudolph Grey's otherwise exhaustive oral history *Nightmare of Ecstasy: The Life and Art of Edward D. Wood, Jr.*

What really captured my imagination about all of this was that apparently a copy of the screenplay was sitting in the archives at Loyola Marymount University. So it wasn't that the screenplay was lost so much as no one had bothered to go get it, yet.

I've been a fan of Wood's ever since I was about 14 years old and I first saw Tim Burton's fanciful biopic *Ed Wood*. There was something about the movie that spoke to me: the way Scott Alexander and Larry Karaszewski's screenplay focused on Wood's eternal optimism and friendship with Bela Lugosi, Johnny Depp's cartoonishly unflappable portrayal, and Tim Burton's keen eye for the look and feel of the era of black and white Hollywood B-pictures all came together to make it what I thought was the greatest film of all time. Funny, since it was about the guy who famously made the so-called *worst* movie of all time, *Plan 9 From Outer Space.*

My interest in Wood only grew when I read *Nightmare of Ecstasy* and realized there was a whole lot more to the filmmaker than Burton's movie let on, mostly involving the booze-fueled later years of his life working in the early days of the adult entertainment industry, turning out some nudie movies, a couple pornographic features, lots of shorts and a staggering amount of novels, short stories, and magazine articles.

Ever since the early days of my Wood exploration, I've always wanted to make some kind of contribution to his world, or the world of his scholars and admirers. I just didn't know what that contribution could be. So, my interest faded in and out as the decades went by, and it eventually came back in full force in 2021 when I was stuck working at home in the middle of the unprecedented COVID-19 pandemic.

Suddenly, I had enough time on my hands to reach out, contact and get involved with some of the names I recognized from the Wood community, including Bob Blackburn and Greg Javer, whose words you've read in the previous pages. And, I finally indulged in purchasing some obscure vintage paperbacks Wood wrote that I'd always wanted to own but had never taken the plunge on before, including a copy of *TV Lust* from Wood's own personal collection.

It was about that time that I started thinking about *The Frank Leahy Legend* sitting in an archive at LMU. I suddenly realized if I wanted to contribute something original to the world of Wood, that screenplay would be my way in. Under normal circumstances I would have gladly visited LMU to take a look at the real thing. I envisioned myself putting on a pair of those protective gloves and carefully leafing through it in an isolated research room like the reporter in *Citizen Kane* or like I'd see my own dad do in his own academic research. Thanks to the pandemic, this was not to be. But also thanks to the pandemic, this meant that LMU would agree to send a digital copy of the screenplay in lieu of a personal visit.

Normally I would have made a note of this in my head, got home from work, and promptly forgotten to follow up on it. But since I was working from home I had the luxury of immediately following up on it before I had the chance to thwart myself. I contacted the archives via their website, got a fairly prompt response, and arranged to have the screenplay emailed to me. When it arrived, I was surprised to find that the library had sent me all 145 pages of it, instead of just a small sample, as they had said they were limited to. It was my lucky day, and I set about reading a work of Ed Wood's that likely no one else had read since maybe 1975.

Before I got the screenplay, the primary questions I had in mind were, one, whether or not it would turn out to actually be a screenplay by *the* Edward D. Wood, Jr. of B-movie infamy, or if there was some kind of misunderstanding and, two, if it *was* by the real Wood, would his irrepressible personality and unique style make it into

Leahy's decidedly non-Woodian life story, or would it ultimately read as a work for hire, devoid of Wood-weirdness?

Of course my first question was easily answered right away by the title page. This was undeniably *the* Ed Wood, as evidenced not only by his full name on the cover but also his initials written in his own hand. This made sense, since we already knew the screenplay was on Wood's résumé, but I had prepared myself for a letdown just in case. Turns out, it wasn't a letdown.

We'll address my other questions in the pages to come, but when I was done reading the screenplay I had a whole new set of questions. More than ever I wondered how Wood, an underdog who wore his quirks on his (angora) sleeve ended up writing about macho, win-at-all-costs Notre Dame coach and Knute Rockne protégé Frank Leahy? After all, the only mentions of football in Ed Wood lore are about how he hated the game and was begrudgingly watching it the morning of his fatal heart attack. And, after that, how had this screenplay, of all screenplays, found its way into LMU's archives?

Last thing first: LMU had a partial answer for me about the provenance of the screenplay itself. It came from Father Michael Mandala, S.J., of the Blessed Sacrament Church in Hollywood, CA. It was part of a large collection of screenplays, teleplays and other movie memorabilia dating from 1924-2005. The note on the archives website said they don't know for sure how the screenplays came into the church's possession, but the thought is that a parishioner donated them.

The interesting and odd thing about this collection is that Ed Wood's screenplay sticks out like a sore thumb among other much more classic and impressive works – various drafts of *Star Wars* movies, screenplays from the silent era, and tons of names you'd recognize as legitimately important in the world of film – *Raiders of the Lost Ark, My Man Godfrey, Twelve Angry Men…* the list goes on. What's an unproduced Ed Wood screenplay doing in this company?

Ed Wood's résumé said he wrote it for Scotty Williams Entertainment and the screenplay's title page had a copyright notice for Bernard J. Williams, the same man who wrote the book the screenplay was based on. So, there were two leads but both led nowhere.

As my co-author, Greg, mentioned, there was an article in the March 1975 issue of the *Chicago Tribune* that mentioned both *The Frank Leahy Legend* and *The Life of Muhammad Ali* (with Ali playing himself) as two upcoming films that were going to be shot in Chicago by summer with local filming coordinated by Rick Holtzman of Illinois Film Services.

I looked Rick Holtzman up and found him as president of a property management company managing vintage buildings in Chicago. He confirmed he not only worked for Illinois Film Services, he was actually the founding director of the agency. Unfortunately he said that while he remembers meeting Muhammad Ali, he has hardly any other memory of these projects, considering they were almost 50 years ago. So, another dead end, but since Holtzman confirmed having met Ali, I could only assume *The Life of Muhammad Ali* eventually hit cinemas as Tom Gries' 1977 film *The Greatest*, which was shot partially in Chicago and starred Ali, himself.

Back to *The Frank Leahy Legend* author and screenplay copyright holder Bernard Williams. There was some speculation from Greg that maybe he didn't exist at all. Maybe it was a pseudonym for a ghostwriter – a ghostwriter who may have been Wood himself. The book was published by an outfit called JCL Services – could they have hired Wood to make the whole thing up? I wasn't so sure about that, though I had a moment when I took a look at other copyrights in Williams' name.

There are many Bernie Williams in the world, but one born in 1913 wrote something called *Fillers for Employee House Organs*. A "house organ" is a term that refers to an in-house magazine or other publication published by a company for its customers or employees. "Fillers" were little stories, quotes and anecdotes that would be used to fill up the pages of these kinds of publications. That seemed like the kind of thing the author of *The Frank Leahy Legend* would have written – the book is full of little apocryphal anecdotes that seem shoehorned in and have little to do with Leahy himself.

What I saw next blew my mind: this Williams had also written a series of short stories about a character named Sister Mary Agatha. The Catholic connection was the first thing that struck me, not as a Wood thing but as a Williams-Leahy-Notre Dame thing, but what I noticed next was some of the titles appeared to be potentially suggestive: *Sister Mary Agatha and the Bastard*, *Sister Mary Agatha and the Class Reunion*, *Sister Mary Agatha and the Questionable Behavior*, *Sister Mary Agatha Does a Little Business* and last but not least, *Sister Mary Agatha and the Running Back*.

For a moment I thought I was looking at a list of pornographic nun short stories written by Ed Wood as Bernard J. "Bern" Williams. Or were they simply cute anecdotes about a nun character you might find as fillers in a "house organ" for a Catholic organization? I was probably reading too much into it.

If this was the same Williams, he apparently also wrote for *Reader's Digest* and the *National Enquirer*, was a columnist for the Times Publishing Company and hosted a radio show for WRIE-AM, a *sports* radio station in Erie, PA. He died in 2004. That would seemingly make him *not* the same person as Ed Wood. *If* this was even him – his bio in *The Frank Leahy Legend* refers to him as a businessman, industrialist manufacturer, inventor and merchandiser, but nothing about writing or radio. Then again, this was printed in 1975 and a lot can happen between 1975 and 2004.

Greg found one last Bernie Williams clue when researching a couple sci-fi magazines, *Galaxy* and *Worlds of If*, for another project. These magazines featured stories written by authors repped by the late Forrest J. Ackerman, a man most famous now as the prototypical horror and sci-fi fan, and creator of *Famous Monsters of Filmland* magazine. Ackerman also repped Wood, for a time. Greg was astonished to see a familiar name listed as associate publisher in a May, 1970 issue of *Worlds of If* — Bernard Williams. Is it possible that Williams, working with a variety of sci-fi writers who knew Ackerman, was turned on to Wood by Ackerman himself? Of course, we don't even know if this is the right Williams, and we may never know. But it's an intriguing possibility.

All this time I had been working off of an original copy of *The Frank Leahy Legend*, though I noticed Greg was working off of a re-published version of the book that came out in 2009 called *Iron Desire: The Legacy of Notre Dame Football Coach Frank Leahy*. Along with Bernie Williams, this book listed a K. Raven Rozier as author and copyright holder. Looking for more info, I decided to reach out to her. She's a busy person but got back to me quickly and graciously answered several of my questions.

She said her husband was JCL out of Torrance, CA. JCL Services is listed as the publisher of *The Frank Leahy Legend*, and Greg and I had already been trying to figure out what exactly this outfit was. Some kind of military contractor was all we could figure out. The way she phrased it made me wonder if JCL was literally her husband's initials, but Rozier said that wasn't the case, and that she doesn't know what it stood for. She did confirm the company did military contract work and it required her husband to get classified clearance (much like Wood's work with Autonetics in the 60s – maybe a connection there?) but that she didn't know specifically what he did for the military. I was curious if JCL Services ever published any other books and Rozier said she didn't know of any. She said her husband passed away three years ago (2017ish) so she couldn't go to him with any of these questions.

When asked how she came to re-publish the book and renew the book's copyright, Rozier said she's a writer and her husband asked her to rewrite the book for him, and had her re-register the copyright as part of that request. When she went to rewrite the book, she decided instead of rewriting it she'd just do a little editing because she found the language and "retro vibe" charming.

Interestingly, she had never heard about the Ed Wood connection to the book, or about any screenplay at all. She said it was fascinating, though, and that she did know her husband had some business ventures in the entertainment industry and figured he might have come across Wood there, but that was just a guess. She said Bernie Williams was her husband's business partner, and that her husband had told her stories about both Williams and Leahy, but never mentioned Wood.

Williams claims to have written the book from hours and hours of interview tapes between Leahy and himself. This made me wonder if, in editing the book, Rozier had listened to the tapes. She said she had never heard them. I asked if she ever saw them, thinking maybe they were stored in an attic or basement. But no, she had never seen them, either. She did say she had a photo somewhere of her husband with Williams, but wasn't sure where it was.

When asked about Scotty Williams of Scotty Williams Entertainment, Rozier said she thought he may have been Bernie's son. The book and screenplay both mention a Bernie, Jr. and the book mentions Bernie's daughters, but no Scotty. Maybe Scotty was his brother, or a son the book doesn't mention. We may never know.

As far as how the screenplay got to Blessed Sacrament, Rozier said maybe Williams' family donated it to the church upon his death, but that was just a guess. I'd had the same thought, but while I knew Williams would have easily had a copy of the Wood screenplay, I wondered if he had a giant and impressive collection of seemingly every notable screenplay in Hollywood history.

I was reaching the end of my leads but decided to look into Blessed Sacrament directly. The Catholic church is right in the middle of Hollywood, about a 10 or 15 minute walk from Ed Wood's last apartment before his final eviction. Wood probably would have been aware of the church, but most likely would not have gone there, being a Protestant. Still, the church's central location to all-things-movies meant it had a long history with a lot of big names, making it likely any number of parishioners could have easily dropped a cache of screenplays on them. Notably, the first professional organization for screenwriters and actors, early versions of the screenwriters' and actors' guilds, were formed there.

Bing Crosby was married there, John Ford's funeral was held there and the list goes on. According to Wikipedia, the 1958 B-list horror western *Teenage Monster* (also known as *Meteor Monster*) had a scene shot on the church's steps. A cursory scan of the movie doesn't make this seem likely as most of it appears to take place in a stock western town. The movie was directed by Jacques Marquette, though, who was DP on *The Christine Jorgensen Story*, a funny Ed Wood coincidence considering Wood's own *Glen or Glenda* was originally intended to capitalize on the famous sex change case. On the other end of the spectrum, the only movie listed on the Internet Movie Database as using Blessed Sacrament as a location is *L.A. Confidential* – a decidedly classier affair than *Teenage Monster*.

I finally decided to just ask Blessed Sacrament directly – did they have anything in their records about where they got this screenplay collection that they donated to LMU? I got through to someone at the church on the phone who gave me an email address to contact but after a few tries I never heard back. Today, Blessed Sacrament is known for its community outreach programs including a gay and lesbian ministry and assistance for the poor, so they probably have more important things to do.

As Greg always says, we'll figure it out some day. But for now, there are still a couple really big question marks about how Williams connected with Wood and how this screenplay ended up in the archives. What is certain, though, is that we can now finally read it and get a little more insight into the life and art of Edward D. Wood, Jr.

1st DRAFT

SCREENPLAY

9/1/75 $8,000

" THE FRANK LEAHY LEGEND "

Original Biography by

BERNARD J. WILLIAMS

Screenplay by

EDW. D. WOOD, Jr.

The Feature Presentation: *The Frank Leahy Legend*

by Edward D. Wood, Jr.

Commentary by W. Paul Apel

Right from the get-go, we've got a lot of interesting stuff to look at here. First, we see that this is the first draft of the screenplay. It is also the only known draft in existence, and I'd wager the only draft that was ever written, though that's just a hunch based on Wood's usual style.

It looks like Wood either finished the script or handed it over to whoever commissioned it on 9/1/75, a little over a month before his 51st birthday and only a couple years before he died. The scribble next to the handwritten date reads "EDWJ" for Edward Davis Wood, Junior. At first I wasn't sure if this was handwritten by Wood himself or not, but there are many sources for his handwriting and when I checked his inscription in his own personal copy of *Diary of a Transvestite Hooker*, it became clear that this was, indeed, Wood's own handwriting, a fact made obvious by the many characteristic flourishes.

Judging from the copy of the screenplay I received from LMU, it is difficult to tell if I have a scan of a photocopy, or a scan of the original hand-typed, hand-signed document.

The "copywrite" (sic) notice at the bottom of the title page is dated 1976 and credited to BJW, obviously the initials of the author of the biography the screenplay was based on, Bernard J. Williams. The date and the font/style of the notice make it clear this was added to the cover page after Wood handed it off.

Although I don't know the specifics behind how Wood came to get the job, I can make a guess from an interview with filmmaker Ed De Priest how much Wood may have been paid for this screenplay, and how quickly he probably wrote it. According to De Priest, Wood wrote the 1969 caveman sex film *One Million AC/DC* for him for $500 over the course of only a couple of days. *Leahy* might have been a more complex job for Wood, not only because it was more than just a few lines here and there between sex scenes, but also because, as we read on, it becomes clear that Wood did not simply open the book and do a page for page adaptation. He actually created his own structure and used bits and pieces of the book throughout – some things that appear early in the book appear late in the screenplay, for example. So, he would have had to read the book, taken some notes and then written the screenplay, which may have taken him longer than a couple days. There are even several pages of locations and characters at the end, which, in an age before screenwriting software or word processors, would have taken time and effort to compile as accurately as Wood has.

On the other hand, maybe the work period wasn't *that* much longer than Wood's usual, judging from the way the screenplay's quality starts to dip pretty quickly.

1st DRAFT

SCREENPLAY

"THE FRANK LEAHY LEGEND"

Original story

BERNARD WILLIAMS

SCREENPLAY

EDW. D. WOOD, Jr.

1. EXT. FOOTBALL HALL OF FAME - LONG SHOT - ESTABLISHING - DAY

Establishing the footballers place of honor. There is no one else around except a tall, heavy-set man and a young boy who walk to and enter the building.

2. INT. HALL OF FAME - MEDIUM WIDE - MOVING - DAY

The CAMERA MOVES with the man and young boy, BERNIE and young BERNIE WILLIAMS. They pass the busts of the football greats and finally the father stops the boy in front of the bust of FRANK LEAHY. Both are silent for a long moment, the father almost reverent. The boy finally looks up to his father.

YOUNG BERNIE
Was he really that great dad?

BERNIE
(pats his head)
You better believe it.

YOUNG BERNIE
You wrote a book about him, huh!

BERNIE
(nods)
I wrote the book.

YOUNG BERNIE
Can I read it?

BERNIE
(grin)
I dnn't think you'd understand just what you were reading...not for awhile

CONTINUED

Framing Device

Ed Wood never met a framing device he didn't like. His films are full of them. It has even been said *Glen or Glenda* is a film that seems to re-start every ten minutes or so, each time with a different framing device, as what should be a fairly straight forward story gets told in an increasingly convoluted manner – first by Bela Lugosi as a god-like mad scientist, then by Timothy Farrell as Dr. Alton, and so on. *Plan 9 From Outer Space* offers bookends and narration inexplicably provided by TV psychic Criswell, who returns in a few other films either written or directed (or both) by Wood as a character within the story who also narrates. Even one of Wood's pornographic films, *The Young Marrieds*, features voiceover narration from a god-like observer.

These are only a few examples, but they all tend to take on a similar pompous, pretentious, self important, know-it-all tone that is seemingly at odds with the low-rent B-movie shenanigans unfolding on the screen before us.

Here, Wood has chosen a framing device that differs from the book he has been asked to adapt, which shows that he instinctually knew one of the first rules of screenplay adaptations, which is to deviate from the source material as much as you can to make a movie, not a re-formatted book. So, you can see from the outset that he has put some thought into this and isn't just on autopilot.

In this case it is a subtle difference, but a definite one. Here, Wood has the author of *The Frank Leahy Legend*, Bernie Williams, as a character in the story, telling the story to his son. In the source material, Williams is very much present as the voice telling the story, but the story is told from the point of view of him going to visit Leahy and conducting interviews with him. The story of Leahy's life unfolds as a conversation between Williams and Leahy, with many asides and unrelated anecdotes.

Inspiration for Wood's choice of framing device involving a child marveling at a Leahy statue at the Football Hall of Fame may come from one of the many illustrations in the original book – one appears near the end of the book, depicting just that: a child gazing in wonder at a bust of Leahy. Aside from this illustration, no scene like this appears in the book.

FL - 2

2. CONTINUED

BERNIE (cont'd)
yet anyway...Maybe...maybe if
I told you about him...
(pace change)
Come on, let's find someplace
to sit down.

He takes the boy's hand and they start back in the direction from which they had come.

3. EXT. HALL OF FAME - WIDE - DAY

The two come out of the hall of fame and find a comfortable spot beneath a shade tree where they sit down.

4. CLOSE TWO

BERNIE
His whole name was Francis William
Leahy...

START SLOW
DISSOLVE

5. EXT. LEAHY FARM - NEBRASKA - WIDE - ESTABLISHING - NIGHT

All the windows are lighted, but there is an ominous silence which tells of things to come. BERNIE'S VOICE comes over.

BERNIE (o.s.)
...and he came into this world on
the chilly night of August 28th,
1908 in a place called O'Neill,
Nebraska.

The silence, except for a light wind and the rustling of trees takes over again...for a long moment...Then there is the sound of what might be a loud slap then the wailing of a baby's first cries....

6. INT. LEAHY FARM - NEBRASKA - LIVING ROOM - WIDE - NIGHT

A rustic but extremely clean furnished with farm furniture of the period, oil lamps, etc.

CONTINUED

A Life Has Begun

Wood has written Frank Leahy's birth as an almost miraculous, legendary moment in American History. It's not quite on the level of Jesus in the manger, but you could be forgiven if you mistook this description as maybe something out of *Young Mr. Lincoln* as a larger than life American hero comes into the world in a modest log cabin. Okay, Wood doesn't go so far as to call it a log cabin, but the Leahys' Nebraska farmhouse is described in such a way that he must have welcomed the comparison.

This is all Wood's imagination firing at 100% in these early pages – there's nothing in the source material about Leahy's birth. The silence, the wind rustling, is all pure Wood, earning his money by being as dramatic and cinematic as possible right out of the gate. To his credit, so far, this is not a hack job, but an honest try.

FL - 3

6. CONTINUED

The elder LEAHY has been nervously pacing the floor. He stops as he realizes the cries of the baby. He still wears the overalls and work shirt that he had used during the day and his supper is still untouched on the table. He stands, nervously wringing his hands as he looks to the bedroom door. Young GENE and MARIE sleepily rubbing their eyes come down the stairs and look to their father.

GENE

Has it come?

LEAHY SR.

Get back upstairs.

MARIE

When do we get to see it?

LEAHY SR.

Get back upstairs, and I mean that...

This time the kids do as they are told, but their moveback up the stairs and out of the scene is slow. Just as they are out of the scene the rustic door to the bedroom opens and the MIDWIFE comes out. She carries a basin of water and some dirty towels.

LEAHY SR.

Well...? Well...?

She passes him by heading for the kitchen. She glances at his untouched food.

MIDWIFE

Land, you'd think you'd be used to such things by this time... Look there, you ain't even touched what I cooked for you.

LEAHY SR.

Damn it woman...tell me.

MIDWIFE

(as she disappears into kitchen)

It's a boy, just like you wanted.

LEAHY SR., waits no longer, he quickly crosses the room and enters the bedroom.

It's a Boy, Mr. Leahy

The midwife reveals to Leahy Sr. that his new child is a boy, just like he wanted. There's nothing in the source material about Leahy's father specifically wanting a boy, but a parents' preference for a specific gender of a child is a continuing theme in Wood's work. Some sources claim this is an autobiographical detail – Wood's mother wanted a daughter, so would dress Wood in girls' clothing, which eventually led to his adult life as a cross dresser. Wood's father did not approve. This is reflected most famously (or infamously) in *Glen or Glenda*, but appears time and again throughout Wood's work.

FL - 4

7. INT. BEDROOM - NEBRASKA - WIDE - NIGHT

A single oil lamp lights the rustic room. LEAHY SR., slows his movements after he has closed the Behind him. He crosses the room to where his lovely wife, several years younger than himself, lays cuddling the newborn baby in a soft blanket. She uncovers the face momentairly but he reaches down under the blanket and takes the hand out. It is quite large for a newborn.

LEAHY SR.
To hell with his face, it's the hands he's going to use to be a boxer...and look at the size of them...

He beams broadly.

8. INT. BARN - WINNER, SOUTH DAKOTA - MEDIUM - DAY

FRANK is about 5 or 6 now and he is throwing everything into his punches as he dives them into the palms of his older brother GENE. LEAHY SR., is circling telling them what to do...

LEAHY SR.
Use that right, use that right. Hit him with all you got. You know you got more power in that right. Keep your head down just like he was throwing them back at you...that's the way boy... God...I know I've got a champ in a few years...

9.9. EXT. HOUSE - MEDIUM - WINNER, SOUTH DAKOTA - DAY

MRS. LEAHY dressed in her best including a hat, comes out of the door and calls off toward the barn.

MRS. LEAHY
Frank...Gene...it's time for church and a good Catholic is never late for mass.

10. INT. BARN - MEDIUM - DAY

The boys stop their action and LEAHY Sr., pats his

CONTINUED

From Nebraska to South Dakota

The opening narration recounts how Leahy was born in Nebraska. However, the family's move to Winner, South Dakota is handled only in a scene description by Wood, and not articulated by a narrator or a title on screen. So, if you picture this as a movie unfolding before you, you'd have no idea the jump from Leahy's birth to Leahy at the age of 5 or 6 (handwritten corrections here change the original typewritten ages, 6 and 7 – a strange correction considering a big upcoming scene actually took place when Leahy was 3, according to the book) is also a jump from Nebraska to South Dakota.

On its face, this isn't necessarily important – plenty of biopics gloss over little details like every single town a person lived in growing up, only focusing on it when it's important. However, in this case, it *is* important, both in the established "legend" of Leahy as well in this very screenplay, as we'll learn a few pages later.

Since Leahy's entire life story is synonymous with the notion of winning at all costs and his legacy is all about the records he set with winning football teams, it became part of his story that he's the "winner from Winner" – Winner, South Dakota, that is.

Unfortunately, as an audience member watching this never-produced movie, you'd have no idea the family has moved to Winner. This is the first sign of Wood starting to go on autopilot, after a few initial pages of legitimate imagination and attempts at cinematic structure.

FL - 5

10. CONTINUED

black jacket and ties his string tie. He starts out.

LEAHY SR.
Come on boy.

GENE
Right behind you Pa...

LEAHY SR. goes out of the barn leaving the door open.

FRANK
I hate this barn. It stinks.

GENE
Pa always wanted the biggest
barn around these parts. It MAKES
him important or some-
thing.

He has put on his black jacket and straightens his own tie. He crosses to the door as he puts on a rounded black hat.

FRANK
Yeah! Well maybe if it wasn't
around I wouldn't have to do
all this box matching stuff.

GENE laughs.

GENE
Don't count on it.

FRANK, with all the disgust his little mind can muster looks all around the place, to the hay on the floor and in the lofts...

11. EXT. THE HOUSE - WINNER - WIDE - DAY

LEAHY SR., drives the double seated buggy around from the back of the house. It is pulled by their white horse, LIGHTNING. MRS. LEAHY turns to give daughter MARIE last minute instructions. Ann and Eileen with Gene get into the buggy.

MRS. LEAHY
Now you keep a good eyes on young
Frank. You know the kind of mis-
chief he can get into.

CONTINUED

Don't Count On It

"Don't count on it," is a common enough phrase, uttered here by Gene, Frank Leahy's older brother. But Wood fans that read this line can automatically hear Loretta King's delivery of the same line as reporter Janet Lawton in Wood's 1955 film, *Bride of the Monster*, in which this dialogue exchange takes place:

CAPT. ROBBINS
There are no such thing as monsters. This is the 20th century.

JANET LAWTON
Don't count on it. Monsters, I mean.

This is one of the more famous examples of Wood's idiosyncratic, off-the-cuff writing style, as if he wrote the "Don't count on it" retort, noticed mid-typing that it looked like Janet was questioning which century it was, and added the "monsters" clarification just so he could move on without burdening himself with little nuisances like rewriting.

Here, Gene's rejoinder makes more sense, but it's fun to be reminded of Wood's other work and wonder if Wood might have even been referencing himself. Due to the fact that the expression in question is incredibly common, I wouldn't count on it.

Call Me Lightning

Here we're introduced to the Leahy's horse, Lightning, who will become important to the story soon enough. For now, it is interesting to note that the horse, while also important in the source material, goes without a name. Wood was a huge fan of Westerns, and although his usual go-to name for Western heroes was Tom Mix, whose horse was named Tony, here he has taken Western hero Tim Holts' horse's name, Lightning. I'm not sure if there's any proof Wood was specifically a fan of Holt, but he was a fan of Orson Welles, and Holt did take a break from the Westerns to act in *The Magnificent Ambersons*. He also has a very memorable role in the classic *The Treasure of the Sierra Madre* where he holds his own as Bogart puts on a master class.

Wherever Wood may have gotten the name Lightning, it is interesting he felt the need to name the nameless horse from the Williams book.

FL - 6

11 CONTINUED

MARIE
I will mama...I'll keep my eyes
on him every second.

MRS. LEAHY
But if something does go amiss
you run and get Mr. Pugh. And
I'll say the prayers for you
in the church.

LEAHY SR.
Now who's looking to be late
for mass.

She gets into the buggy and they drive off. MARIE watches them then when they are gone, she looks to the barn and sighs, then hands on hips as she has seen her mother do so often she uses her best orders.

MARIE
Frank Leahy, you come right
over to this house right now.

12. LONG SHOT - ANGLED

From behind MARIE to the barn. For the moment there has been no response from FRANK.

MARIE
(shouts again)
You hear me?

FRANK slowly comes out of the barn and makes his way to her. He kicks dust up in front of him and has his hands dug deep into his pockets.

FRANK
I want a glass of milk.

MARIE
I wish Pa would get a bigger
buggy so we could all go to
church and I wouldn't get stuck
with you...You know where the
milk is.

FRANK walks into the house through the kitchen door.

FL - 7

13. INT. KITCHEN - MEDIUM - DAY

FRANK has entered and the screen door snaps shut behind him. He walks across to the ancient wooden ice box and opens the door. He takes out the pan of milk then pours some into a glass he has taken from the sink. He replaces the pan of milk and closes the ice box door. He leans back against the sink and tilts his head back as to drink the milk. The liquid never reaches his lips. His eyes bug at what catches his attention.

14. CLOSE - P.O.V.

There is a box of wooden matches on top of the old wood burning stove.

15. MEDIUM

FRANK lowers the glass from his lips. He doesnt bother to look as he puts it on the sink behind him. His eyes have not left the object which has captured his fascination...the o.s. matches.

16. WIDER

Taking the stove into the scene. FRANK slowly, but deliberately, with spaced steps makes his way to the stove. He glances once back toward the screen door, then takes down the matches and quickly stuffs them into his pocket. He takes the shirt tails out of his pants and lets them drap over the pocket to hide the bulge. He cautiously approaches the screen door and looks out.

17. P.O.V.

Through the screen door to the outside. She is heading toward him with a pail of water.

18. MEDIUM

MARIE comes through the screen door and goes to a bucket at the sink. She pours the fresh water into it. FRANK opens the screen door and she glances at him.

MARIE
Where are you going?

CONTINUED

FL - 8

18. CONTINUED

FRANK
Just outside. It's hot in here.

MARIE
You didn't finish your milk.

FRANK
Ohhh...

He goes back to the sink and gulps down the milk. He puts the glass down to be washed.

MARIE
And don't you go no further than the well.

FRANK
Yeah...yeah...I know.

He goes out.

19. WIDE - THE HOUSE AND THE BARN

As soon as FRANK is outside he makes his way cautiously into a position where he cannot be seen through the screen door he skoots for the barn. It is a quick run and the door is closed just as quickly behind him.

20. INT.KITCHEN - MEDIUM - DAY

MARIE is humming as she begins to prepare something for the others to eat on their return from church.

21. INT. BARN - MEDIUM - DAY

FRANK looks around the place much as he had done before but the disgust is even more prominent...then his eyes light on something else.

22. P.O.V. - CLOSE

A set of boxing gloves hung on a nail beside an unlit oil lamp.

FL - 9

23. MEDIUM - PAN

The CAMERA PANS FRANK across to a position below the gloves. He has to turn a pail upside down and stand on it to reach the gloves. He gets them and jumps down off the pail. He only gives the gloves the briefest of a glance then tosses them to a pile of loose hay. He takes little more time in getting out the matches, lights one and tosses it to the hay which ignites immediately. He throws the remainder of the box into the gaining fire and they soon explode. The fire shoots upward and spreads around quickly. FRANK stands transfixed. But he does not move until he is sure that the boxing gloves are securely engulfed in flame. Then coughing from the steadily increasing smoke he bolts for the barn door.

24. EXT. BARN - MEDIUM - DAY

The doors burst open and along with a tremendous cloud of smoke and amist chickens and pigs and whatever else was in the barn FRANK races out. Coughing, he falls to the ground several times but always regains his footing and races off...His final fall he has twisted his knee slightly and although he can keep up a steady run to safety there is still a slightly limp to his movements.

26. INT. KITCHEN - MEDIUM - DAY

The sound of the chickens, pigs, etc and falling timber finally captures her frightened immagination...she races to the screen door and flings it open.

27. EXT. HOUSE & BARN - WIDE - DAY

MARIE has come out and is looking off to the burning barn where the fire is now burning through the sides and the roof. Nothing on this earth could save the barn at that moment....HOLD FOR EFFECT...FRANK is standing near the house looking back to the barn, his hands dug deep into his pockets but there is no other sound from him except an occasional coughing from the smoke....

DISSOLVE
THROUGH TO:

A Barn Burner

Here begins Wood's dramatization of Chapter II of *The Frank Leahy Legend* – "Burning Down the New Barn." Wood's retelling takes the basic framework of the story told by Frank Leahy to Bernie Williams in the book, but fills in a lot of detail. Sometimes the detail is unnecessary and other times the detail is exactly the kind of stuff a writer *should* add when adapting a story.

For example: in the book, Leahy is left with his sister Marie watching him while the rest of the family goes to church. He already knows where the matches are kept and as soon as Marie looks the other way, Leahy grabs the matches, goes out to the barn, and burns it down. In the screenplay, there's a lot of back and forth and lingering detail of Leahy getting a glass of milk, and in the midst of getting it, discovering the location of the matches. There's no reason why a screenplay that's attempting to cover a man's entire life should linger so much on someone getting the milk out of the fridge, the fact it's in a milk pan, pouring it in a glass, putting it back, taking a sip, leaving it half drank, going back to drink the rest after his sister admonishes him. All that stuff takes up precious real estate and contributes nothing.

However, what *does* work in this section is the fact that Wood dramatizes the discovery of the matches and Leahy being drawn to them. This is exactly the kind of thing a writer should want to dramatize when taking a quick anecdote and attempting to turn it into a story – create some suspense, use a little foreshadowing and draw the audience in.

That's a small example, but here's a bigger one: in the book, Leahy tells Williams he has no idea why he burnt the barn down. So, there is really no motivation behind the story, let alone a moral to it. It's just something that happened.

In the screenplay, Wood works overtime making the story relevant. It still has no moral, so in that sense, it is true to its source material. But it definitely has motivation. The storyteller in Wood starts to build a plot (something lacking in the book) by creating tension between father and son. Leahy's Dad wants him to become a boxer, which is true to the book, but Leahy *hates* boxing, which is less true to the book. In the screenplay, most of his training takes place in the barn, so he associates the barn with boxing, and even articulates if the barn wasn't there anymore, maybe he wouldn't have to box (prompting Gene's aforementioned "Don't count on it.").

When Leahy goes to burn down the barn, in the screenplay, he first sets the boxing gloves, which happen to be in the barn, on fire. The fire spreads and goes out of control, and the barn burns down. Narratively, so far, this is much more satisfying – the boy is motivated to destroy his father's pride and joy (the barn) to avoid having to become what his father wants him to become (a boxer). So what we see here, again, is not just Wood slapping together a screenplay to pocket some drinking money, but actually attempting to construct a coherent plot, which is above and beyond his usual call of duty.

FL - 10

28. EXT. BARN AREA - CLOSE - PAN TO WIDE - DAY

The CAMERA PANS from the horse LIGHTNING, then the buggy, and on to MR. PUGH and some other neighbors, GENE, ANN EILEEN, MARIE and MRS. LEAHY, to end with LEAHY SR., his face stern...other farmers from the area can be seen here and there. The CAMERA PULLS BACK TO A WIDE. The barn is nothing more than smoldering, smoking ashes. LEAHY SR., slowly turns to glare at MARIE.

LEAHY SR.
You were to watch him while we were at church.

MARIE
I did...I did...I did....
(almost in tears)
But he...he...he....

MRS. LEAHY puts a comforting arm around her young daughters shoulder....

MRS. LEAHY
We can't be too hard on her Leahy!

LEAHY SR.
I can be as hard on her as I will it Mrs. Leahy...

He suddenly turns to face all the others and his eyes travel to all of them as he speaks.

And before I put the blame to my family, where it damned well belongs...I gotta' say this... This morning is the last mass I will ever attend in my life. I will never attend a church ever again...

He turns and walks out of the scene, heading back toward the house....

FADE TO:

FL - 11

29. INT. LEAHY KITCHEN-WIDE - MORNING

Mrs. Leahy and Marie are serving the others around the large wooden table. There is a pleasant table cloth over the top of the table but the chairs are rustic. LEAHY Sr., speaks as MARIE serves him. He does not look to her but directly at MRS. LEAHY across on the other side of the table.

LEAHY Sr.
See if you can't find some extra chores for Marie...get her mind sharpened up again.

FRANK, seated to his father's right looks to him.

FRANK
Pa...

LEAHY SR.
What is it son?

FRANK
You shouldn't be so hard on Marie...not when you know what really happened.

LEAHY SR.
And you know what really <u>did</u> happen?

FRANK
Yes sir.

LEAHY SR.
Okay. So let's hear what really <u>did</u> happen.

FRANK
Well...it was like this...You see... This great big wolf snuck down the hill and into the barn, with big fire coming out of its nose. That must be how it started...

MRS. LEAHY
(laughs)
With an imagination like that young Frank is going to go far in this world...

CONTINUED

The Boy Who Cried Wolf

In both book and screenplay, the barn-burning story ends almost identically, with one minor adjustment. Both end with Leahy's parents blaming Leahy's sister, Marie, for the fire, because she was the one in charge of watching Leahy. Leahy, feeling guilty for his sister taking all the blame, comes to her rescue by telling the "truth" of the fire's beginnings to his parents – a giant fire-breathing wolf did it.

Here comes the difference: in the book, Leahy's parents laugh it off, just glad Leahy wasn't hurt, and his father comments with an imagination like that he should be writing comic books. In the screenplay, Leahy's parents laugh it off, but Leahy's mother observes, "With an imagination like that young Frank is going to go far in this world…" (note the ellipsis, a piece of punctuation so beloved and abused by Wood that there's nary a piece of his dialogue that exists without it).

The distinction here is, again, Wood is desperately attempting to steer the story in some direction relevant to the over-arching theme of the movie – Leahy's legend and legacy. The "comic book" comment in the book, while it may be a true recollection of Leahy's, does nothing to advance the story of Leahy's life. The "going far in this world" comment Wood gives Leahy's mother in the screenplay at least points the story in a forward-moving direction, not just hinting at Leahy's eventual greatness, but also moving us along with at least a little momentum. Also, note the comment that brings this episode to a close is given to Leahy's mother by Wood, not his father, setting up the dynamic popular in Wood's work of the mother being more supportive of the son than the father.

All of this, by the way, is in the face of a story without a moral. Usually, the story of the boy who cried wolf has a payoff where the boy cries wolf one too many times, and by the time there is a real emergency and he tells the truth, no one believes him. So the moral of the story is don't lie or else people won't believe you when it matters. Here, there's no payoff, and the only moral that can be gleaned from the pages to come, if the reader wants to try to find one without the help of Leahy, Williams or Wood, is that Leahy continues to cry wolf throughout his life, and it always works out for him as a net positive – so when all else fails, lie.

FL - 12

29. CONTINUED

GENE shakes his head. The other kids surpress giggles and LEAHY SR., sighs. Then they are all served.

LEAHY SR.
I may have sworn never to enter a church again, but we are still going to give our blessings for the food the Good Lord provides us to eat...Bow your heads...

They all do as they have been directed.

30. MONTAGE OF SCENES

YOUNG FRANK and sometimes with his brother GENE go through a series of odd jobs...shoveling snow, selling newspapers or delivering them since the community is so small and wide spread, sweeping out the local tavern or general store, picking fruit trees, helping to plow, etc., (TO THE DISCRETION OF THE DIRECTOR,) and throughout the MONTAGE the boys are growing into their teens.

31. INT. HIGH SCHOOL BASKETBALL COURT - WINNER - WIDE - DAY

FRANK in basketball uniform is shooting perfect shots to the basket. His HIGH SCHOOL COACH comes in from an o.s. area and stands at the end of the court for a moment watching. Then he starts his approach...

32. MEDIUM TWO

FRANK prepares for another throw just as the COACH comes up beside him. FRANK continues the toss and the ball goes out of the scene.

HIGH SCHool coach
You've had one terrific season Frank.

FRANK
(grim)
We lost a couple.

CONTINUED

To the Discretion of the Director

This is not the first time we'll come across "To the discretion of the Director" in this screenplay. Here, Ed uses it to fill out a montage he's describing. In some ways it is redundant – he has fairly completely described the montage and therefore doesn't really need to leave anything to the director's discretion.

On one hand, this might be Wood the writer putting himself in the shoes of whoever might end up directing this picture. Knowing it wasn't going to be him, he was extending some creative license to whoever it might end up being.

On the other hand, it reminds me of something I once read about Wood's screenplay for the pornographic film *Necromania*, a movie he also directed. In Rudolph Grey's *Nightmare of Ecstasy*, actor Ric Lutze says of the screenplay, "The script would say, 'go into sex,' and then you had to make it all up yourself. The script itself was probably only 20 pages long."

Now, this isn't quite the same thing, but it's similar. What we have here is Wood's shorthand as he again starts to shift into autopilot, after initially really trying on this screenplay. Sort of a, "You get the picture," kind of comment used to avoid wasting time doing annoying writer stuff like trying to describe things. You'll see it pop up more and more in the coming pages.

FL - 13

32. CONTINUED

HIGH SCHOOL COACH
You didn't!

FRANK
I'm out only to win!

HIGH SCHOOL COACH
Which is the fighting spirit.
Frank. You'll be graduating
here one of these days. You keep
up the kind of work you're doing
in your studies and in the game
and I've got surprises in mind
for you.

FRANK
The only thing I want after I
graduate from here is someway
to get to Notre Dame. It's all
I dream about...

DISSOLVE TO:

33. INT. FRANK & GENE'S BEDROOM - WINNER - MEDIUM - NIGHT

FRANK is pasting news clippings into a large scrapbook.

34. ANOTHER ANGLE

To take in the pages of the book over his shoulder as
he flips through them. They are all clipps of Notre
DAME wins and stories about KNUTE ROCKNE...

35. MEDIUM WIDE

MRS. LEAHY opens the door. She does not come in but
frames herself in the doorway.

MRS. LEAHY
More on Mr. Rockne and Notre Dame?

FRANK
(looks to her)
Yes, Ma.

CONTINUED

I'm Out Only to Win

This line is a good example of the odd syntax that more often than not finds its way into Wood's writing. Try saying it out loud: "I'm out only to win." Doesn't really roll off the tongue, does it? A more natural line might be something like, "Winning's all I care about," or, "All I wanna do is win." You could even be as lazy as just flipping two words around and still come out ahead: "I'm only out to win."

"I'm out only to win," seems like a robot or an alien attempting to approximate what they think a human might sound like. It's the kind of thing that Wood might catch on the next draft and change, if he ever wrote one, which he probably didn't.

Still, like many things in this screenplay, it stands out as both an example of Wood's problems and an example of his strengths at the same time: it is true that Leahy *was* only out to win, and it's important that this makes it into the main character's mouth, sometime early in the movie, as a sort of thesis statement, so we, as an audience, know what he's all about, and what to expect for the rest of the movie.

Enter Notre Dame

The school synonymous with the name Frank Leahy finally enters the picture, somewhat out of the blue. The opening framing device doesn't set up Notre Dame at all, and nothing in the main action of the story does either. Out of nowhere, teenaged Frank Leahy just blurts, "The only thing I want after I graduate from here is some way to get to Notre Dame. It's all I dream about."

Here, Wood violates the age old "show, don't tell" adage, hallowed among writers. If Leahy's been dreaming this all his life so far, why not show us that? Instead, Wood does things backwards: puts the line in Leahy's mouth, then follows it up with dramatized examples.

It's also interesting to note that, according to Williams' book, Notre Dame was put on Leahy's radar by his high school coach. In Wood's version, Leahy mentions Notre Dame to his coach first, not the other way around.

FL - 14

35. CONTINUED

MRS. LEAHY
You really like that school,
don't you?

FRANK
University, Ma...University.

MRS. LEAHY
University...college...school...
some difference. Your dad and I
didn't see much of anything where
schooling was concerned.
(sigh)
Come on downstairs. Your dad
wants to see you.

She turns and goes back out of the doorway and out of the scene. FRANK closes the cover of his scrapbook, stands up and mirrors his mother's movements.

36. INT. KITCHEN - MEDIUM - NIGHT

MRS. LEAHY has not come into the kitchen and LEAHY SR., sips some coffee from a mug until FRANK, who is very big for his age, comes into the room. The elder LEAHY stands up beaming brightly...

LEAHY SR.
Frank boy, I've got a real
surprise for you.

FRANK
Seems like everybody has surprises
for me today.

37. INT. BOXING BARN - EXTREME CLOSE - POSTER - NIGHT

There is a large poster attached to one of the walls. On the poster is the picture of one of the ugliest, big men one could imagine and the legend reads:

$100.00
TO ANY COMMER WHO CAN PUT
OUT
THE MIGHTY
SILENT JOE BLAHA

The noise of the crowd is heard over this shot, then the CAMERA SWISHES TO A BLUR AS IT CROSSES TO....

Mirroring Mother

There is a very strong possibility that Wood didn't mean anything consciously when he typed, "FRANK closes the cover of his scrapbook, stands up and mirrors his mother's movements." It's probably just Wood's typically awkward way of saying Frank follows his mom out the door.

That said, analyzing the work of a cross dresser who often brought the relationship between sons and mothers into the cross dressing equation in the rest of his work, the choice of words here is striking – "mirrors his mother's movements."

Casting Choices

Now that Leahy has reached his late teens in the screenplay it's tempting to wonder who would have played him if the movie had ever been produced. Usually in films like this, even if multiple actors play the lead throughout his childhood, when you settle into the late teens, early twenties, you usually settle into the star that is going to play the character for the rest of the movie. That's how you get the likes of Gary Cooper, Robert Redford and even Howard Stern playing teenagers, so they can play adults later on.

In his original book, Bernie Williams claims Frank Leahy's own choice to play the lead was Richard Dix, Jr., son of Richard Dix, an actor probably most famous for his Academy Award-nominated lead role in *Cimarron*. Doing a little research I think Williams got it confused – Richard Dix *did* have a son named Richard Dix, Jr., but he died in 1958, long before Williams and Leahy ever met, let alone began discussing a filmed version of *The Frank Leahy Legend*.

However, Dix, Jr. had a twin brother, Robert Dix, who was still a working actor in the 1970s, as he had been throughout the 50s and 60s, with 1956's *Forbidden Planet* probably being his best known film. This is probably who Williams (and Leahy) had in mind. Sure, he would have been in his 40s by the time the movie would have started shooting, but what better age to play both young and old Leahy?

Interestingly, Robert Dix also starred in 1958's *Frankenstein's Daughter*. The makeup artist on that flick was none other than Harry Thomas, who worked closely with Ed Wood on many of his most well known films: *Glen or Glenda*, *Jail Bait*, *Plan 9 from Outer Space* and *Night of the Ghouls*. He even worked on *The Bride and the Beast*, which Wood wrote but did not direct. This puts Leahy's number one choice, Robert Dix, in pretty close proximity to someone proven to know Wood. It's tempting to think maybe that's the bridge that got Wood the gig, even if it was over 20 years later. Then again, Harry Thomas has 104 makeup department credits to his name on IMDb, so who knows.

I get strong Scott Bakula vibes when I see portraits or photos of Frank Leahy. Of course he would have been too young for the part in the 70s and is too old for it now, but it probably would have worked in the early 90s, as proven by his turn as a football player in *Necessary Roughness*. The other name that comes to mind is Jason Sudeikis, but I guess he's already busy playing another football coach.

FL - 15

38. EXTREME CLOSE - TO FULL

The head of SILENT JOE BALAH. He even looks uglier and darker in person than his poster picture had depicted.

After a moment of establishing the CAMERA suddenly ZOOMS bACK to take in the extreme barn arena. A make-shift ring has been set up in the center of the ring and the crowd is gathered thickly around it. Featured among the onlookers are a TIMEKEEPER, REFEREE, and BLAHA'S MANAGER who stands next to the TIMEKEEPER. All are waiting for the opponent.

39. MEDIUM CLOSE - TIMEKEEPER & FIGHT MANAGER

The MANAGER leans in to the TIME-EEEPER.

MANAGER
Just keep in mind that Balah can't talk or hear. But he can sense when the three minutes are up and he will look over here, so you got to give him a signal...Got it?

TIME-KEEPER
Got it!

40. WIDE

The REFEREE climbs through the ropes and goes to the center of the ring. He holds up his hands for silence, and the audience obeys...although the drinking continues.

REFEREE
Gentlemen, the bout you all have been waiting for. The height of our July 4th celebrations...

There are no women in the audience.

That's this here boxing match between the celebrated Silent Joe Blah....
(points to Balah)
And our own....

The crowd has booed Balah, but in anticipation of the next name the boos change to cheers...The REFEREE points in the opposite direction...

FRANK CANE.....

CONTINUED

Blaha vs. Balah

So begins Wood's adaptation of Leahy's account to Williams of his boxing match with "Silent" Joe Blaha, who Wood first refers to correctly but then begins calling Balah on accident for the rest of the sequence.

In this instance, comparing the book to the screenplay shows Wood's mind is getting a little muddled. The details are the same – Leahy's father arranges a bout between Leahy and deaf pro boxer, Blaha, that takes place in a barn on the 4th of July. The point of the story, however, is clearer as told by Leahy to Williams. Basically, Leahy's getting destroyed in the fight and the ref and timekeeper agree to ring the gong ending the round early if it looks like either fighter is in trouble. Blaha, being deaf and therefore unable to hear the bell, has been trained to look to his manager at the end of a three minute round to get a visual cue that the round has ended. But when the round ends early, Blaha keeps fighting, and Leahy wins by foul. Blaha's manager protests that it's an unfair call due to the shortened round, but he and Blaha are run out of town.

As you can see, this is already a pretty convoluted story, but Wood, who may have been several drinks into a bender as he typed away, loses all track of what's going on, and although he does his best to dramatize the scene, it is difficult for a reader to pick up exactly what's supposed to be going on without re-reading a few times.

So, this is another example, albeit an oblique one, of Leahy crying wolf – he beats a pro in a boxing match by exploiting his opponent's deafness, a tactic that would normally be viewed as un-sportsman-like but here is presented as another example of Leahy continuing to be a "winner." Before reading Williams' book, I wondered if Wood was deliberately attempting to undermine Leahy's macho image with stories like this, but after reading it I'm not sure what to think except that Leahy really did believe in the value of winning "at all costs" – literally, not figuratively.

I also wondered if "Silent" Joe Blaha was even a real boxer, and it turns out he was. According to BoxRec.com, which bills itself as Boxing's Official Record Keeper, Blaha was a middleweight boxer whose career lasted a short three years, from 1925 to 1927. He hailed from Omaha, Nebraska, just as Leahy says, and only has three fights on record, all three of which he lost. None of them were in Winner, South Dakota on the 4th of July, but I guess if it's true he fought 16-year-old Frank Leahy in a barn circa 1924, it probably wouldn't be on record, anyway.

FL - 16

40. CONTINUED

It is FRANK LEAHY who LEAHY SR., and GENE lead into the ring. FRANK wears green velvet trunks.

SPECTATOR
Hey, we know who is who...let's get the thing going!

DRUNK
(staggered)
Yeah...

Other ad-libs to the same value.

REFEREE
Okay Lehhys outta' the ring.

Frank forgetting his change of name starts to leave with his father and brother, but his father spins him back to the center of the room and BALAH meets him there.

REFEREE
Okay, so touch gloves and go at it...

The REFEREE has no more then stepped back when BALAH lands a solid one on FRANK'S jaw. He goes down.

REFEREE
One...

FRANK staggers to his feet and spits out a bloody tooth.

41. MONTAGE.

More of the same. FRANK stays on the ground for more of the count each time. The big, dark man slams him again and again. FRANK gets in several good punches but they mean little to the outcome of the fight, or so it would appear. The fight continues (<u>TO THE DISCRETION OF THE DIRECTOR</u>.)

42. MEDIUM TWO - TIME-KEEPER AND REFEREE

The REFEREE leans in and whispers to the TIME-KEEPER.

CONTINUED

Tooth Loss

Emphasis is placed here on Leahy spitting out a bloody tooth, and in pages to come we'll see tooth loss becoming a recurring theme that Wood seems to linger over whatever chance he gets.

Although this specific tooth loss is mentioned by Leahy in Williams' book, it is tempting to play armchair psychologist here and wonder if Wood's own potentially traumatic tooth loss was sometimes on his mind, when writing scenes like this. It's unknown how exactly he lost his front teeth – his tall tale was reportedly that they were lost at the butt end of a Japanese soldier's rifle in World War II, but James Pontolillo's fantastic book *The Unknown War of Edward D. Wood, Jr.* has some other interesting suggestions and evidence that this is probably not true.

To the Discretion of the Director part II

Here's another one, this time as soon as sports action starts. Increasingly, throughout, Wood's good with non sports scenes but as soon as it comes time to describe some actual athletic action cinematically, he checks out and leaves it to the director, answering the question, "What did Ed Wood know about sports?" with a resounding, "Not much."

FL - 17

42. CONTINUED

REFEREE
Frank's losing steam. When I get back in the center ring the bell.

The TIME-KEEPER nods.

43. WIDER

BALAH is hitting FRANK hard and FRANK is covering himself as best he can with his arms protecting his face. The REFEREE begins to circle them. The BELL sounds. FRANK drops his guard but the deaf/mute BALAH hasn't heard the time called. He lands several more blows until the REFEREE parts them and points to the bell.

The REFEREE lifts FRANK'S hand high in the air.

REFEREE
Frank [illegible] Cane is the winner by a foul....

BALAH'S MANAGER jumps into the ring...

MANAGER
The hell you say. That was no three minutes. My man couldn't hear no bell. What in hell are you hicks trying to pull around here?

LEAHY SR., AND GENE jump into the ring and others' start doing the same...The REFEREE points this action out to the MANAGER and the startled BALAH who doesn't understand what has happened.

REFEREE
I'm only the Ref. Why don't you argue your point out with them.

LEAHY Sr., holds out his hand to the MANAGER, palm up. The MANAGER angered, but fearing for his life through physical numbers reaches into his pocket and peels off a bill. He slaps it into LEAHY SR., hand, then he shoves his fighter toward the ropes and they make their way out of the ring and the barn amid the laughter of the audience and the ad-lib congradulations showered upon FRANK.

FADE TO:

FL - 18

44. INT. FRANK AND GENE'S BEDROOM - MEDIUM TWO - NIGHT

They are ready for bed, but not in bed. They sit on each of their beds and look across to each other. FRANK is real down; dejected.

FRANK
(touching his jaw)
Nobody can say I have the jaw of a fighter. I figure I don't have a jaw for anything.

GENE
Come on, you can't say that. You put on a great show out there tonight.

FRANK
I stunk!

GENE
All that matters is that you won...think about that. You made Pa mighty proud.

FRANK
How can you say that was a win?

GENE
The betters that were putting their winnings in their pockets would dispute your attitude. Look! You're a Leahy. You can be anything you want.
(surveys Frank's cuts)
So...maybe you won't be a fighter...but you don't want to be a fighter.

FRANK
Dad's counted on it so much. I'd hate to disappoint him.

GENE
Look! Football...baseball, those are your games. Maybe not baseball as much as football, maybe I'm just the other way around. Up at State the coach told me I was damned good except for my forward pass... But that's because my hand has been broken five times.

CONTINUED

Finally, Football – Sort Of

This is a nice scene between Leahy and his brother Gene, emphasizing Wood's strength for advancing the plot through dialogue, contrasted with his weakness for clearly communicating complex action sequences.

Notably, 18 pages into the screenplay (which would translate to roughly 18 minutes into the hypothetical film), football is finally mentioned. We've had Frank Leahy shooting hoops on the basketball court and sparring in the boxing ring, but not one mention of football until now, unless you count the Football Hall of Fame.

When Leahy was born, his father grabbed his newborn "big" hands and says they're perfect for a boxer. Now, Leahy's brother grabs his 16-year-old "big" hands and says they're perfect for football.

FL - 19

44. CONTINUED

GENE reaches over and lifts FRANK'S big hands.

GENE
Those are football hands.

FRANK
(grins)
You think so Gene?

GENE
I know so! One of these days Dad and all his friends, everybody in the world will be reading about Frank Leahy, the winner from Winner.

FADE TO:

45. INT. DANCE HALL - WINNDER - NIGHT

W wild probition era type of dance hall where the liquor is secreted in places supposedly where raiding parties would not look for it...dancing, the guys and their dolls doing their thing...small band blaring out the music. If the drinking is more genteel the liquor is taken in coffee mugs. If taken from the bottle the bottle is slipped from inside of jackets, pockets and purses. We can also see that some of the girls have flasked which shape to their legs and held there by fancy garters. (ALL TO THE DISCRETION OF THE DIRECTOR).

FRANK is seen standing near the main entrance. His arms are crossed over his chest and he is attempting to look as mean and as tough as possible. His eyes keep roving over the entire rowdy room.

46. MEDIUM - TO A TABLE

A young THIN MAN and a PRETTY GIRL with coffee cups in front of them are laughing it up and drinking. She suddenly burps then giggles...

PRETTY GIRL
'Scuse me honey. I gotta visit the powder room...quick...

CONTINUED

The Winner from Winner

Gene makes the first mention of Frank Leahy as "The Winner from Winner," a moniker he was known by in real life – because he grew up in Winner, South Dakota and had a winning record with Notre Dame (and other schools).

Unfortunately, as mentioned before, Wood has dropped the ball here – because I'm reading the scene headings, I know Leahy now lives in Winner, South Dakota with his family. But if I was in a matinee audience watching this unfold onscreen, this would be the first mention of "Winner" so far and, out of context, it wouldn't be immediately clear what Gene is talking about. After all, it's not as if "Winner" is a common name for a town.

So, a line Wood probably wanted to be impactful would fall flat, without a proper rewrite.

However Much I Booze

Notice the extreme detail Wood lavishes on the drinking in the dance hall scene. It's not just a passing mention that it's the Prohibition era and people are sneaking drinks. Nope, we get a list of different ways people are sneaking their drinks, and of course close attention paid to women's garters. Drinking and women's clothing: two of Wood's favorite subjects. As opposed to, say, sports.

FL - 20

46. CONTINUED

He indicates her dismissal with a wave of his hand then the same hand dips inside his coat for the flask. The girl, unaided, leaves the scene.

An obvious DRUNK at a table behind this couple has been eyeing him throughout the previous dialogue. He staggers to his feet and topples the chair over behind him.

47. CLOSE - FRANK

Catches the sound and he looks off carefully, expecting trouble.

48. MEDIUM - TO THE TABLE

The DRUNK grabs the THINNER MAN roughly by the shoulder and spins him around which almost causes his chair to fall to the floor.

DRUNK
Hey Mac, I don't like the way you been puttin your hands on my girl.

THIN MAN
I don't even know who your girl is, friend.

DRUNK
Wise guy, huh!!!

He pulls the THIN MAN to his fist and throws a wild punch into his jaw. The blow knocks the THIN MAN across his own table...The DRUNK reaches over and pulls him to his feet.

49. MEDIUM - TO FRANK

He quickly leaves his position at the door, moving in the direction of the action.

50. MEDIUM - TO TABLE

Other patrons have gathered around, cheering on the fight as FRANK pushes his way through them. The DRUNK has just sent the THIN MAN across the table again and the table crashes under him, as FRANK grabs the DRUNK with

CONTINUED

FL - 21

50. CONTINUED

both his big hands.

FRANK
Come on buster...OUT!!!

The DRUNK who's hands are free catches FRANK off guard with a good one to his mouth. His lip begins to bleed and he spits out a tooth. That's all FRANK needs. He grabs the DRUNK by the seat of his pants and his collar and....

51. WIDER

...gives him the bums rush to the front door. He bodily tosses him to the....

52. EXT. DANCE HALL - MEDIUM - NIGHT

...street. The DRUNK lands heavily on the sidewalk and lays there a moment wondering what happened as FRANK comes out and stands over him. FRANK waits for another offensive. But it doesn't come. The DRUNK slobbers to his feet and staggers off down the street muttering threats about the next time...

53. ANGLED

FRANK moves back to sit on the bottom step of the four steps that lead to the dance hall. It is then that CLAYTON his team mate, CLAYTON, from high school comes up with tö lovlies, a BRUNETTE and a BLONDE.

CLAYTON
Thought you didn't want to be a boxer.

FRANK
(spitting)
Hell. I just got enough money to get that tooth put in and the bastard knocked it out.

BLONDE
You hurt bad, honey?

FRANK swells up...a pride in his job.

CONTINUED

Tooth Loss part II

Although this is becoming a theme not just in this screenplay but also in Wood's work as a whole, it is important to note here that this tooth loss incident is also accurate to the source material. Looks like Leahy and Wood suffered some of the same traumas.

In fact, this entire episode is a fairly accurate retelling of a story Leahy tells in the Williams book, right down to the reason the two drunks are fighting in the dance hall in the first place.

Writers working on adaptations are forced to make a lot of decisions when it comes to what to gloss over, or combine together, or linger on or even totally delete or totally create out of thin air, and they always have their reasons. I wish I knew Wood's reasoning for the things he recreates faithfully here and the things he glosses over. My best guess is that he lingered on the things he had a personal connection to – simple things like getting into a fight or partying in a dance hall – and skips over things he doesn't care about – like sports.

FL - 22

53. CONTINUED

FRANK
A bouncer is supposed to be able to take anything...all in the line of duty.

CLAYTON
Say! If you can still drink through that lip come on and lift a couple with me and the girls.

FRANK
First round is on me.

He rises to stand with them. The music becomes loud through the door again and they all look to it. The BLONDE goes sort of ape. From their entrance the BLONDE has had all eyes for FRANK. She locks his arm with hers...

BLONDE
I'd just love to dance...with you.

BRUNETTE
(squints)
My feet are killing me.

CLAYTON
Maybe you should take your shoes off, honey!

He quickly reaches to the hem of her dress and lifts it.

I'll even help you.

She pulls away giggling.

BRUNETTE
You say the silliest things sometimes Clayton.

The others watch her as she exposes her well turned ankle and takes off the shoe. CLAYTON suddenly reaches over and takes the shoe from her hand.

CONTINUED

FL - 23

53. CONTINUED

CLAYTON
(backing uP)
Down the field for a pass, Frank!

FRANK runs off some distance down the street. The girls are amazed; don't know what to expect from this sudden movement from the boys.

CLAYTON makes an excellent pass and FRANK catches it, tucks it under his arm and races in for the touchdown. The girls get it, laugh and clap as the boys rejoin them.

CLAYTON
Nobody can beat the team of Clayton and Leahy...

LEAHY
Correction! Leahy and Clayton.

CLAYTON
(feigned, downcast)
Whatever!!!

LEAHY
And these two grêats will lead Notre Dame to even greater victories in the future...

The BLONDE hugs FRANK'S arm even tighter as she snuggles in to him.

CLAYTON
(sigh)
There goes that Notre Damne bit again.

FRANK
It's the way I feel...and that's where I'm heading if my scholarship comes through. Coach Walsh seems to think it's cinched. Wouldn't you go?

CLAYTON
That's a big football school and tough...why be a small fish in a big pond. Let's go to South Dakota Normal.

CONTINUED

Quarterback Princess

You can imagine the thrill of getting to this passage from the point of view of a Wood enthusiast, searching for Ed Wood among the pages of a sports biopic. We finally get to the first scene of anyone playing football of any kind, in what is ostensibly supposed to be a football screenplay, and what are they using as a football? A woman's shoe!

As this scene first unfolded before me, I couldn't believe it. Of course, Wood would take something he doesn't relate to at all, football, and write about it through the lens of something he actually cares about – women's clothing. Take the one thing most centrally important to Leahy's life and substitute it with the one thing most centrally important to Wood's. It was beautiful.

And, it turns out, too good to be true. To my surprise, this entire passage is faithfully recreated from Williams' book, as told to him by Leahy himself, right down to the high heel football substitution. This might hint at the idea of Wood as potential ghostwriter for Williams. Maybe his involvement with the project began before the screenplay? Of course, there's no proof of that, so it's probably just a happy coincidence.

Scholarship

This is the first mention of Leahy having a potential scholarship to play at Notre Dame, and coach Walsh seeming to think it's cinched. A more traditionally structured screenplay would have included some set ups for this declaration instead of letting it come out of nowhere, the same way a character like Clayton might be introduced a little earlier instead of suddenly rocketing to prominence for one scene. There was a little hint of a set up in the previous scene with the then-unnamed Coach Walsh, on the basketball court, in which Walsh hinted at a "surprise" for Leahy – a hint that never paid off in subsequent pages. Perhaps that surprise was this scholarship opportunity and Wood forgot to follow up on it?

FL - 24

53. CONTINUED

FRANK
Naw...My mind has been made up for a long time...ever since I can remember.

They start for the doors.

BRUNETTE
Where is Notre Dame?

CLAYTON
Who knows?...Could be California for all I know....

FRANK laughs and they push open the doors to the dance hall and enter.

FADE TO:

54. EXT. LEAHY HOUSE - WINNER - WIDE - DAY

FRANK and brother TOM are sitting on a bench near the kitchen as a PAPERBOY riding a small cart behind a year-worn horse rides by. He shouts a greeting to the boys as he tosses a newspaper to them. TOM is about ten years old. FRANK gets up and goes to the folded paper. He picks it up and quickly unfolds it to the sports page. He let's the rest of the paper fall to the ground. He beams as he reads and TOM comes up beside him.

TOM
Something good, huh Frank, huh?

FRANK
You bet. Wait until Gene reads this. Listen...
(excitedly
reading)
"Four horsemen win 16th straight, victory - Rockne Performs another Miracle."

TOM looks over FRANK's shoulder and his eyes grow wide at what he sees.

CONTINUED

FL - 25

54. CONTINUED

TOM
WOW!!! And you're gonna go to that scho...university!

55. REVERSE - TO THE PICTURE

A large picture of the Notre Dame Four Horsemen. They are on matched horses and each wears a leather helmet and carry footballs under their arms. Circled below is a head and shoulders shot of KNUTE ROCKNE.

FRANK (o.s.)
"Outlined against the blue-grey October sky, the Four Horsemen rode again."

56. MEDIUM - ANGLED

Taking in the two boys with the screen door to the kitchen in the background. The elder LEAHY comes out carrying a milking pail. He stops as he hears the words.

FRANK
(reading)
"In dramatic lore they were known as famine, pestilence, destruction, and death. These are only aliases. Their real names are Stuhldreher, Miller, Crowley and Layden."

LEAHY SR., sighs broadly, shakes his head and moves off toward their new barn...a much different style then the one which had been burned down years ago... and it already is showing the years. The boys hear his sigh and they turn to watch his movement. He shakes his head every so often during his move toward the barn. The boys watch him a moment, then again look to the picture in the paper silently.

57. CLOSE - THE PICTURE

...of the four horsemen.

SLOW DISSOLVE TO:

Alias Don Miller

The famed "Four Horsemen" from Notre Dame are discussed here by name, including right halfback Don Miller. They made up the backfield of Notre Dame's 1924 team. They only lost two games the three years that they played together, and they won a National Championship. This was all under the coaching of Knute Rockne, briefly mentioned in the screenplay a few pages earlier, and mentioned again here. He'll become important in a few more pages.

The reason I highlight Don Miller is because of what seems to be yet another coincidence. Wood's pseudonymous director credit for his pornographic film *Necromania* was Don Miller. Assuming he came up with this name himself, it's tempting to think he had Notre Dame's Don Miller fresh on his mind because of the *Leahy* screenplay.

Unfortunately, that's probably not the case. *Necromania* came out in 1971 and Wood completed the *Leahy* script four years later. Williams' source book wasn't even published until 1974. So, for this to be anything more than a coincidence, Wood would have had to have known of Don Miller completely independently of his involvement with the *Leahy* screenplay. While not entirely impossible, given the fame of the Four Horsemen and Notre Dame football in general during Wood's lifetime, it seems unlikely given Wood's seeming lack of interest in all things sports-related.

All four Horsemen made it into the College Football Hall of Fame, but Miller was the last one inducted, in 1970. Maybe Wood glanced at a newspaper in 1970 and saw the name. Then again, it's not as if Don or Miller are particularly uncommon names.

Interesting footnote: there was a 1934 *Three Stooges* short called *Three Little Pigskins* in which the Stooges are mistaken for the famed football players, "the Three Horsemen". One scene was shot on the sidewalk outside 6317 Yucca Street in Hollywood, less than a block from the 6383 address where Wood wrote his *Leahy* screenplay – a one-minute walk, by Google's reckoning.

FL - 26

58. CLOSE - INSERT - ANOTHER NEWSPAPER

A WINNER newspaper with the headlines:

" WINNER UNDEFEATED "

(WALSH) HIGH SCHOOL COACH (o.s.)
We do things a little different here, then at most schools - most schools use the single or double wing, and here we use the Notre Dame Shift...
(nostalgic)
Notre Dame, where I played ball under Coach Rockne, greatest coach who ever lived - you'll be hearing a lot about him...

DISSOLVE TO:

59. INT. SHOWER - HIGH SCHOOL - MEDIUM - DAY

FRANK is standing just outside the shower with only a towel wrapped around his middle as COACH WALSH enters.

FRANK
Hi Coach...congratulations.

WALSH
Hey boy, we'd have been nowhere without you and those big, straight shootin' hands.

FRANK looks around to make sure that no one can overhear his words.

FRANK
Still on Saturday night with those dollies?

WALSH
Be by to pick you up around 7. But keep it down. The faculty ever find out we were taking on students around here they'd hang the both of us.

FRANK
Mumms the word, you know that.

CONTINUED

Winner Undefeated

Finally, a newspaper headline clues us in to the fact that Frank Leahy is the Winner from Winner because the town he lives in is called Winner. Unfortunately at the same time we're introduced to a mysterious voiceover from Leahy's coach, Walsh, who starts getting nostalgic about his Notre Dame days. I say mysterious because it is unclear where this disembodied reminiscence is supposed to come from, or be directed to, or when it was said, or why. It's completely and utterly without context, and while the next scene does involve Walsh as a character, it does not seem to logically follow from this voiceover.

Hello, Dollies

Uh oh. What have we here? Seems all-American hero Leahy and his high school coach are going on double dates together? Walsh's line, "The faculty ever find out we were taking on students around here they'd hang the both of us," makes it clear that, at least in the screenplay, Wood intends us to understand that Walsh is dating a high school student.

Of course, these days it goes without saying that that kind of conduct would land Walsh in jail and, judging from the dialogue, apparently it was frowned upon enough even in the 1920s that Leahy and Walsh have to keep it secret. But what's baffling is that a screenplay intended to lionize Leahy includes this kind of stuff.

On first read, I thought maybe Wood was just writing what he knows – not that Wood was preying on high school girls, but that most of his output at the time of this screenplay's writing was pornographic, and maybe hacky porn plots like coaches hooking up with students were easy for Wood to fall back on if he had to fill some time.

After reading Williams' source book, I now know this was just Wood's attempt to include stuff that's in the book, which is even more baffling. Whatever disinterest or even cynicism Wood may have had towards sports, Williams, by contrast, was an almost religiously devout worshipper of Frank Leahy and Notre Dame, and yet, deemed this kind of stuff appropriate to cover in his biography. It'd be one thing if we're talking a "warts and all" type of story, but this is the Frank Leahy *legend* we're talking about, here. It's so odd that it starts to seem like maybe Williams thought this was something to be proud of.

In any case, the story in the book is slightly different. Leahy still double dates with his coach, which is gross, but it's Leahy who is bagging his teacher (whose full name is given – I checked with the school and someone of this name definitely worked there when Leahy attended), not the coach who is sleeping with students. Leahy says he, his teacher, his coach, and another woman dating his coach, "used to go dancing and to various affairs together, in which many school rules were broken."

59. CONTINUED

WALSH suddenly beams all over and gives FRANK a hefty slap on the back. FRANK rubs the stinging spot.

FRANK
Hey, what's that for?

WALSH
Got some news for you.

FRANK
Good or bad?

WALSH
The best...the very best my boy.

FRANK seems to be puzzled for the moment, but the coache's face suddenly tells it all.

FRANK
You mean...? Come on you can't mean...Yoweeeeee, you do mean....

60. EXT. LEAHY HOUSE AND FIELD - WIDE & LONG - DAY

LEAHY SR., is chopping wood near the kitchen door where a great deal is already piled up. FRANK, astride LIGHTNING can be seen racing across the field. LEAHY SR., looks in that direction as soon as he hears the galloping hooves. FRANK dismounts on the run and lets LIGHTNING find his own way to the barn.

FRANK
Hey Pa...Pa...

LEAHY SR.
(cutting him off)
My name ain't Joe Silent Balah. I'm two feet from you. I can hear perfectly well.Bring it down, boy, bring it down.

FRANK is excitedly trying to get his words out. MRS. LEAHY, attracted by the commotion, comes out through the screen door and stands looking at the two men and drying her hands on her apron.

CONTINUED

FL - 28

60. CONTINUED

FRANK
I got it. I got it. I got the scholarship to Notre Dame!

LEAHY SR.
Ahaaaaaaaaaaa.

He has cut FRANK off and returned to his wood chopping. MRS. LEAHY takes up a laundry basket from the side of the house.

MRS. LEAHY
I'm happy for you son. It's what you want.

LEAHY SR.
What's he know what he wants!
(still chopping)

FRANK goes to hug his mother and spin her around. She drops the basket.

FRANK
Knute Rockne is the football coach there.

LEAHY SR., tosses his ax into the uncut wood as he turns to them.

LEAHY SR.
Football, college, and a fist full of Knute Rockne's won't do you one bit of good in this world. You best get yourself a man's trade... Boxing, that's where champs are made.

LEAHY SR., has started to shout.

FRANK
(ignoring him)
Now I gotta figure about room board, tuition, books, laundry...

LEAHY SR.
Not one red cent will you get from me for such foolishness. Not one cent...not even for transportation.

CONTINUED

FL - 29

60. CONTINUED

EEAHY SR. (cont'd)
Now you see it my way. Go on over to Denny Ryan's in Omaha for two years where you can learn to be the champion boxer I want you to be and I'll pay for everything you need. You won't have to want for one blessed thing. All you got to do is try and you'd be the next Heavyweight Champion of the World. What a proud day that would be for me.

FRANK goes to his father and puts his arm tenderly around his shoulder.

FRANK
Pa, you know I've got a glass jaw! The fight with Balah...my job as a bouncer...they should prove that. I'm not fast on my feet. I get winded quick, and my knees are weak.

LEAHY SR., shrughs FRANK'S arm from around his shoulder.

61. INT. SPEAK-EASY - MEDIUM - NIGHT

In reality a converted cellar, smoky and no pretence at being luxurious. FRANK and COACH WALSH sit in a back booth in a more darker part of the establishment. They have untouched beers in front of them.

WALSH
We're going to miss you around the old school boy. But I'm happy that you got the scholarship.

FRANK
If I hadn't I'd be on my way to Denny Ryan's in Omaha and a career in boxing...

WALSH
Those hands weren't meant for boxing.

CONTINUED

Scholarship part II

Leahy finally has his scholarship, but still thinks he needs money for room, board, tuition and books, none of which his father says he'll pay for, because he wants Leahy to go to Denny Ryan's in Omaha to learn boxing. But, if Leahy's scholarship doesn't cover any of that stuff, what exactly does it cover?

A page later Walsh says he's happy Leahy got the scholarship, and Leahy responds that if he hadn't gotten it, he'd be on his way to Denny Ryan's in Omaha. So something is off here. Let's review: Leahy gets scholarship. Leahy tells Dad he got scholarship, but needs help with money. Dad refuses. Leahy tells Walsh it's a good thing he got the scholarship.

All this doesn't add up, but it's the kind of stuff you end up with when you write something in a couple marathon sessions and never look back at it. Add the possibility of heavy drinking to the mix, and you can see where Wood starts to lose track of his own story.

FL - 30

61. CONTINUED

FRANK
Tell my Pa that.

WALSH
No thanks. I tangled with him just to get you into basketball.

They both laugh...it is not a boisterous laugh...but light and knowingly.

When do you plan to leave?

FRANK
The way I've got to travel... day after tomorrow. That should give me plenty of time to get there for enrollment.

Two pretty girls take up residence at a table near them and they have not missed the ever searching eye of COACH WALSH.

WALSH
Then that gives us time for one more escapade together...

FRANK
Huh...?

WALSH indicates the girls.

(beaming)
Ohhhh.

The men get up and start their move in.

FADE TO:

62. INT. LEAHY KITCHEN - MEDIUM - MORNING

MRS. LEAHY pours a large glass of milk in front of one of two places still set on the kitchen table, then replaces the milk to the ice box. She takes out the egg tray and sighs upon realizing it is empty. She closes the door but keeps the empty container in her hand.

FRANK comes into the room and takes his place in

CONTINUED

PL - 31

62. CONTINUED

front of the milk.

FRANK
Morning Mom...

MRS. LEAHY
Morning Frank.

She takes a step or two toward the screen door, then stops. She does not look back to him.

You're...You're all packed?

FRANK
Since last night.

MRS. LEAHY
Heard you walking around in your room last night.

FRANK
I'm sorry if I kept you awake.

MRS. LEAHY
Oh, no...nothing like that. I couldn't sleep...I've got to get some more eggs. Marie is always putting the empty egg carton back in the ice box.

She then reaches into the pocket of her apron and turns to walk back to FRANK. She hands him a twenty dollar bill.

Your father would be as mad as a hornet if he knew I did this.

Tears begin to well up in her eyes. She turns quickly and goes out through the screen door letting it slam shut behind her.

FRANK gazes a long moment, in silence, at the bill. Then he hears his father's footsteps coming toward the screen door. He puts the bill into his shirt pocket.

LEAHY SR., pushes open the screen door and comes in. He glances at FRANK but for the moment says nothing. He makes for the coffee pot which he carries back to the table. Pours his cup full, returns the pot to the

CONTINUED

Gentle as a Kitchen

This is the beginning of a genuinely touching sequence in which Leahy says goodbye to his parents before going off to college. In the book, Leahy's father refuses to help pay for school and that's it. Wood gives a lightly humorous and human touch to the story by having first Leahy's mother sneak him some money, and then his father do the same, neither of them wanting the other to know they've gone soft.

It's interesting to note Wood seems to zero in on the kitchen scenes, giving characters plenty of busy work – first there was the milk from the barn sequence, but now we have detailed stage directions instructing what Leahy's mother does with the eggs, what Leahy's father does with the coffee pot. Comparing this to the football sequences later, we either have a case of a writer who ran out of steam or a writer who flourishes in familiar domestic situations and fumbles on the gridiron. Maybe it's a little of both.

FL - 32

62. CONTINUED

stove then take his place at the table. He fiddles with the cup without drinking and he still does not look directly at FRANK.

FRANK
Morning Pa!

LEAHY SR.
Hurumppp!

There is a long pause.

FRANK
Ma's gone out to get some eggs.

LEAHY SR.
I saw her...she told me...she was crying.

He then takes up his cup of coffee and sips. When he puts it down it is then that he looks directly to FRANK.

Still going to that...university, huh!

FRANK
Guess I've made up my mind to that.

LEAHY SR.
This morning huh?

FRANK
Yes sir.

LEAHY SR.
You know how I feel about this football business....
(sigh)
But you better damned well make the best football player that ever set down a foot on a field.

FRANK
You've always said, Pa, that a Leahy has to be the best.

LEAHY SR.
You remember that.

CONTINUED

FL - 33

62. CONTINUED

He reaches into his pocket and when the hand comes out it is filled with bills which he stuffs into FRANK'S pocket.

LEAHY SR.
You don't say a word about this to your Ma. She'd think I've gone soft in the head or something.

FRANK grins and puts his hand over his father's as it rests on the table.

FADE TO:

63. EXT. NOTRE DAME - UNIVERSITY - ESTABLISHING - DAY

Several shots of the university...

BERNIE (V.O.)
So Frank Leahy was on his way to Notre Dame...a wish so long demanded of himself was about to be fulfilled. Destiny was beckoning him....

DISSOLVE TO:

64. EXT. NOTRE DAME PRACTICE FIELD - WIDE - ESTABLISHING - DAY

KNUTE ROCKNE is runing his scrimmage. He watches the men work for a moment then blows his whistle for them to gather around him.

65. MEDIUM GROUP

ROCKNE
Miller...get over here!

MILLER, one of the players runs up to the coach.

MILLER
What's up Coach?

CONTINUED

The Return of the Narrator

Bet you almost forgot there even was a narrator or a framing device, huh? Well, Bernie's narrating voiceover makes its triumphant return here, about a half hour of hypothetical screen time since we last heard it. And it's definitely taking on that pompous, authoritarian tone Wood often imbued his narrators with. In case you're wondering, although Williams in his book has a definite voice, it does not match this narration style.

You can almost hear Criswell reading these lines: "…a wish so long demanded of himself was about to be fulfilled. Destiny was beckoning him…." It's reminiscent of narration from *Orgy of the Dead* like this: "Ahh, the curiosity of youth… on the road to ruin! May it ever be so adventurous!"

Narration like this might have come in handy earlier to explain some things like the Leahy family's move from Nebraska to Winner, South Dakota. Maybe that was going to be in the second draft.

Here, the narration seems to signal the end of act one of the screenplay, which, in a traditional three-act structure, would normally end right around page 30. So, Wood's right on time with this shift of action from Leahy's youth to his college days, and a change of scenery from Winner to Notre Dame.

Enter Knute Rockne

Probably the second most important character of the screenplay arrives in a suitably effective entrance, berating his players on the field. It's a well enough drawn character that it seems like it would have been a plum role with the right casting and makes me wonder who Williams, Leahy or Wood might have had in mind. Pat O'Brien played the role in 1940's *Knute Rockne All American.* I wonder if Wood ever saw that movie, and if so, if he had O'Brien's performance in mind as he wrote.

In my experience, the memory of *Knute Rockne All American* only lives on in the "Win one for the Gipper" quote, referring to George Gipp, the character played by Ronald Reagan. This line was popular in the 80s because of Reagan's presidency, but I have to imagine it would have also been in the popular consciousness in the late 60s and early 70s while Reagan was governor of California. In fact, he had just left after eight years in office at the time Wood was writing this screenplay.

FL - 34

65. CONTINUED

KNUTE
What in hell do you think you're doing out there? You can't tell me that's football.

MILLER
Well coach...I...I...

KNUTE
Notre Dame players are always ready. They know what to do in any given situation. A great team has the ability to switch immediately from defense to offense and to start blocking instead of tackling...
(all hard)
Damn it, you just stood there when Carrideo intercepted that pass. What were you doing Miller, saying Mass?

KNUTE ROCKNE might have continued his tirade but the distant sound of galloping hooves comes over the scene.

NOW WHAT THE HELL IS THAT?

Assistant Coach TOMMY MILLS comes into the scne just as the others turn to look off down the field. All are looking now as the hoof beats become louder but still in the distance.

66. LONG SHOT

Down the field. It is FRANK LEAHY steaming up the field toward the assembled group. He is riding LIGHTNING at full gallop, heading for KNUTE and the others. He pulls up in front of them at the same full gallop.

67. CLOSE GROUP

FRANK is beaming all over. He breaths deeply of the air around him.

FRANK
I'm here...I can't believe it... but I'm here. I finally made it.

CONTINUED

Horse Play

And here we have Lightning the horse's starring scene, an appropriately cinematic moment in which Leahy literally rides Lightning all the way from his home and right onto the Notre Dame football field. This is straight out of Williams' book, as told to him by Leahy, though it's the only reference I can find to this incident having occurred.

This story would have us believe Leahy rode Lightning from Winner, SD to South Bend, IN, which is a distance of about 800 miles. Google estimates this to be a 12-hour drive, but apparently a typical, healthy trail horse can travel about 50 miles in a day. So that would be a 16-day ride, except after one day at 50 mph, a horse might have to rest and recuperate for a day or two. So let's say Leahy took it easy and went about 25 miles per day, it would have taken him about a month to get to college. This is around 1928 when cars were not unheard of and trains were the way to go.

So, a month long trip is not outside of the realm of possibility but it certainly does stretch credibility, if only for practical reasons. Assuming Leahy camped out, his only expenses would have been food and water for himself and Lightning, but would a month of those expenses be significantly less than a train ticket?

Of course, this is all ignoring the fact that the entire reason Leahy rides a horse to college at all is because his parents will not give him money, so it begs the question – why, then, would they give him a horse? Wood's screenplay muddies this somewhat, since he actually does have Leahy's parents give him money, which begs a whole other question – why ride the horse, then?

Tall tale or not, this is yet another case where a seemingly cinematic flourish actually turns out to be sourced from the book.

FL - 35

67. CONTINUED

KNUTE PUTS HIS HANDS on his hips and looks around at his other players in utter amazement.

KNUTE
Here that men...He's here...
He's finally made it...Who
the hell are you, Paul Revere?

The players laugh.

MILLS
You heard what the coach asked.
Who are you?

FRANK has been staring in awe at the great ROCKNE. He momentarily evades MILLS' question.

FRANK
You're...You're Knute Rockne...

KNUTE
(to Mills)
That answer your question?

KNUTE throws up his hands and walks out of the scene.

FRANK
(to Mills)
Oh...Oh...I'm Frank Leahy...
reporting for my football
scholarship.

MILLS
What the hell are you doing on
a horse.

FRANK
(Ironic)
Why, I rode him here!

68. CLOSE - KNUTE

Standing back with some other players.

KNUTE
How far did you ride him?

FL - 36

69. CLOSE - FRANK

Some of the other players have come up behind him.

FRANK
(proudly)
From Winner, South Dakota,
Sir...

70. GROUP

KNUTE ROCKNE steps back in close to FRANK and the horse again.

KNUTE
That's a long haul.

FRANK
Yes sir. But I've ridden old
lightnin a lot further before.

KNUTE looks around at the others again, then back to FRANK.

KNUTE
So now that you're here, what
do you plan to do with him?

FRANK
Well I could sell him, but he's
like part of the family. I'll
wire my dad that he's coming
and I'll have him shipped back
collect.

KNUTE
(condescending)
Well that's nice. For a minute
there I thought we might have
to fit him out with a set of
shoulder pads...
(Hard)
Now get him the hell off this
field and park him someplace
then report to Freshman coach
Tommy Mills.

FRANK
Yes sir...I'll do that sir...

He starts to spin LIGHTNING around but stops in the move.

CONTINUED

FL - 37

70. CONTINUED

FRANK (cont'd)
Where do I find Coach Mills?

MILLS
(hard)
That's me...and you better believe it! Now get movin!.

FRANK kicks the horse and races off down the field.

71. CLOSE - KNUTE

Shaking his head still in amused amazement with the sound of the galloping hooves disappearing in the distance.

FADE TO:

72. EXT. DORMITORY - MEDIUM - MOVING - NIGHT

FRANK comes down the steps from his dormitory and starts along the walk way. "MOON" MULLINS comes out soon behind him and just before FRANK goes out of scene he is stopped by MOON'S call.

MOON
Hey...hey...Frank....Frank Leahy!!!

FRANK stops and waits for MOON to join him then with the CAMERA MOVING WITH them, they walk along.

MOON
Heard the coach made you team tackle today.

FRANK
Yeah. Will you get that! A position the first time out.

MOON
With 200 guys or more those first days of the try out I thought it would take the whole first year for the coach to get down to me! I'm a guard!

CONTINUED

Show, Don't Tell

Wood's in violation of this rule again here as he has the information that Leahy makes team tackle his first time out in a line of dialogue, rather than dramatizing the scene on the practice field. This is an example of how Wood has no problem dramatizing something he finds interesting, like a guy riding a horse onto a football field, but skips over stuff he either doesn't know or doesn't care about, like what someone might do in their first football practice to impress Knute Rockne enough to make team tackle.

"Moon" Mullins

Larry "Moon" Mullins, Leahy's roommate and teammate at Notre Dame, is mentioned in Williams' book three times. He hailed from Pasadena, CA and played fullback for Rockne at Notre Dame, going on to a career in coaching.

Interestingly enough, Mullins' nickname, "Moon," is never mentioned in Williams' book, but it is included here in Wood's screenplay. This shows that Wood somehow had some amount of knowledge outside of the contents of his source material. So Wood either chose to do extracurricular research, which shows an impressive amount of dedication to this project, or Williams happened to mention this fact to him or Wood knew more about Notre Dame football going into this job than we've previously assumed (his Don Miller pseudonym then becomes another piece of evidence).

Mullins probably got the nickname "Moon" from a popular comic strip by Frank Willard that ran in papers from 1923 to 1991 called *Moon Mullins*. The titular character was a wannabe boxer staying in a boarding house, always broke and in need of cash for his various misadventures in the world of vice.

Mullins later went on to play himself in 1931's *The Spirit of Notre Dame.*

FL - 38

72. CONTINUED

FRANK
You really thought you'd make it, huh!

MOON
Well sure...didn't you?

FRANK
You bet I did. I've known it since I was...oh....that high!

He show's a child's height with his hand.

What's that building over there, the one with the stuffed hawk.

MOON
That's Washington Hall...upper-classmen...and the hawk is their mascot.George Gipp stayed there...

FRANK
The Gipper...the one Rockne made famous in his game speech that day...

MOON
That's the one...

FRANK
I read about it in the Winner, papers.

MOON
Only one thing...The Gipper made himself famous...Rockne only made sure nobody forgot it...But don't get it wrong. My brother bunked with him and he knew. Gipp was a real man's man. He wasn't what you could call a sait off the football field. Not that guy... Why he could out cuss a sailor. He liked his booze, the girls... He gambled good and he was one of the best pool hustlers around. Rockne just let it slide...after all he was the best player he ever had...

CONTINUED

The Gipper

George Gipp played halfback and quarterback and punted for Rockne and Notre Dame before dying young and inspiring Rockne's most famous speech, "win just one for the Gipper," which was immortalized in the film *Knute Rockne All American* starring Pat O'Brien as Rockne and Ronald Reagan as the Gipper.

In Williams' book, Leahy quotes Rockne as saying Gipp, "was one of the finest gentlemen I ever knew…"

This stands in stark contrast to the treatment Wood gives Gipp here. None of this information about Gipp cussing, boozing, womanizing, gambling and pool hustling is in Williams' book – it's all unique to Wood's adaptation and seems to fly in the face of his treatment in Williams' book, which seems like a dangerous thing to do if you're writing something for hire. Still, there's evidence Williams got as far as location scouting for this script, so it must have been okay with him.

According to the December 30, 1991 issue of *Sports Illustrated*, where Gipp's former teammate Heartly "Hunk" Anderson was interviewed, Gipp was indeed a pool hustler and poker player, and even bet on football games, probably including Notre Dame ones. However, Anderson also says though he was popular with women due to his looks, Gipp seemed to keep them at arm's length and prioritized his gambling over dating.

That didn't stop a 2007 exhumation of Gipp's body to confirm whether or not he had a child out of wedlock with a woman who would have been an 18-year-old high school student at the time of his death. The result was that he was *not* the father.

So, add this to the mounting evidence that Wood had knowledge of this material independently of Williams' book. Going into this project I would have assumed Williams' book was the one and only thing Wood had ever read about Notre Dame, but that increasingly seems not to be the case.

Why did Wood feel compelled to include this aside about Gipp, considering it was not part of Leahy's story? Is it a deliberate attempt to demythologize these legends, or does he just find it interesting? Perhaps some residual annoyance with Governor Reagan motivated it. We'll probably never know.

FL - 39

72. CONTINUED

FRANK slaps MOON on the back.

FRANK
Up until now...

MOON gets the point and they both laugh.

MOON
Yeah, guess that's right...
And when we do get that famous
maybe Knute Rockne will let
some things slide for us too.

FRANK
Yahooooo...bring on the girls.

Laughingly they move on down the walk. The CAMERA STOPS and HOLDS on them.

73. REVERSE

The two men walk in towards the CAMERA and then FRANK stops...looks off. MOON catches his gaze and looks in that direction.

74. ANGLED - GOLDEN DOME

Notre Dame's Golden Dome.

MOON (o.s.)
That's the Blessed Virgin Mary...

75. CLOSE TWO - FRANK & MOON

Looking.

MOON
You can see her from anwhere on
campus. They also say, she sees
you,also, and that forever, wherever you go for the rest of your
life she's looking over you, all
because you're a Notre Dame man.

FADE TO:

FL - 40

76. INT. RECREATION ROOM - MEDIUM CLOSE - NIGHT

on a MOVIE SCREEN where we can see stock footage of a vintage game. The players are in the uniforms of the period. It is played in the real rough and tumble style of the period with little or no rules...every man for himself. There is off scene laughter...then the lights come on...as the film flickers to the end.

77. WIDE

During ROCKNE'S long speech there willbe INTERCUTS of the men with their expressions...serious, humor, etc., (TO THE DISCRETION OF THE DIRECTOR).

ROCKNE
And there you have it gentlemen.
The golden days of 'mass-en-tackle'.
'Bout the only time you saw the
football was when the referee
thrw it in. The eleven heaviest
men became the squad.
(laughter)
The single wing, the double wing,
and then the one which really
opended up the game where you
could really see what was going
on. That was the Notre Dame
Shift.
The Shift brought on the Four
Horseman. I take it you all
know who they were!
The average Horseman weighed 157
pounds...
(doubles up his
fist emphasizing)
Smart! Fast! Trim-ankled!
And now what are they trying to
do to us? They're tryin' to drag
us back to cow-minded, hippopotamus-
chassis-type football with big
dull clod-hoppers sufferin' from
Charley-horses between the ears.
(again laughter)
Now we gotta' problem this year.
The rules tell it that on the Notre
Dame Shift, the offense must come
to a stop and remain in position
for one full second before the
ball is passed. Well, we'll stop
for a full one-and-two-tenths

CONTINUED

Stock Footage

This is the first of several times Wood mentions stock footage in the screenplay. This time, since Rockne is supposed to be showing old timey football footage, the literal use of stock footage makes sense, but in the pages to come, Wood suggests using stock footage for several scenes a normal production would actually shoot – specifically, for some of the in-game football action.

This is worth mentioning because Wood's use of stock footage is one of his most famous and identifiable traits as a filmmaker. The odd juxtaposition of stock images with the footage he actually shot often resulted in giving his movies a strange, other worldly, dream-like feeling, making it difficult for an audience member to figure out exactly what is happening, where it's happening and what the relationship between two shots is meant to be, contextually.

Famous examples include the buffalo stampede used to represent emotional turmoil in *Glen or Glenda*, the octopus footage juxtaposed with a prop octopus in *Bride of the Monster* and the endless shots of the military in *Plan 9 From Outer Space.*

Did Wood specifically suggest the use of stock footage simply because he was so used to using it himself, and was just writing the screenplay from experience? As a writer for hire who wouldn't have to worry about any of the aspects of the film's actual production, he could have easily just included scenes of big audiences or complex action on the field without bothering to suggest stock footage. Or, did he include notes about stock footage just as a helper for whoever did end up making the film – a suggestion on how to save money?

There is the possibility Williams instructed Wood to write the screenplay with certain budget considerations or limitations in mind, which would explain the mentions of stock footage and the constant cutting away from sports action. But Wood's own style would explain this as well, so it's hard to tell.

Rockne's Monologue

Here's an impressive monologue for Knute Rockne, including a whole bunch of realistic-sounding football jargon. Sadly I probably know less about football than even Ed Wood, so I can't weigh in on whether or not this makes any sense, but I did verify the Notre Dame Shift was a thing (a thing that was outlawed, by the way), and single wing and double wing are actual things. The Shift is mentioned once in Williams' book, but single wing and double wing are not, so again, Wood either already knew the basics or did a little above and beyond research so he could give Rockne appropriate things to say.

FL - 41

77. CONTINUED

KNUTE ROCKNE (cont'd)
seconds, just to keep our enemies happy, even though I know we couldn't keep them happy if we stopped for all of five seconds, because their objection is not to the Shift; but to us. Our trousers have gotten too big for them...Well, we're going to beat the hell out of them anyway...RIGHT?

78. WIDE AND ANGLED

ALL
Right!!!

79. ANGLED - TO KNUTE

With FRANK FEATURED in the foreground.

KNUTE
Well, if we don't it won't be long you'll see a Notre Dame team with bovine expressions and ox-knuckles ankles predominating. ...And by the Lord, the fellow with the mustache on the sidelines doing his best to give an air of strategic cunning... That will be me!

FRANK has been featured above all the others through out KNUTE ROCKNE'S dialogue during Scene 77.

DISSOLVE TO:

80. EXT. CAMPUS NEAR PRACTICE FIELD - MEDIUM - PAN - DAY

It is Autum and the trees are shedding their leaves. KNUTE ROCKNE in extremely deep thought, hands behind his back is walking along one of the campus walks. The sound of practice maneuvers comes over. KNUTE stops and looks off. His eyes study what they see.

FL - 42

81. LONG SHOT- TO THE PRACTICE FIELD

Action (TO THE DISCRETION OF THE DIRECTOR)

MILLS
Good, Culligan. Alright you offensive tackles come on over here.

FRANK and HAGEN run over to him.

82. CLOSE GROUP - FRANK, MILLS & HAGEN

MILLS
Let's check your stances... Hagen!

HAGEN assumes his position.

MILLS
Good!

HAGEN rights himself...

MILLS
Now you Leahy!

FRANK assumes his stance...

83. CLOSE - KNUTE

Studying closely.

84. CLOSE GROUP - FRANK, MILLS & HAGEN

FRANK still in the position. MILLS walks around him.

MILLS
Move your hand to the right a bit..a little more...keep your back straight and your feet further apart...you better do some more ankle exercises... Okay....

FRANK stands up, rubs at his back.

FL - 43

85. CLOSE - KNUTE ROCKNE

KNUTE
(calls off)
Tommy!

86. CLOSE - TOMMY MILLS

TOMMY
Yeah Coach.

87. LONG SHOT

From behind KNUTE.

KNUTE
Come over here a minute.

MILLS leaves the others and runs the distance to KNUTE.

TOMMY
What's up Coach?

KNUTE
Try Leahy as Center.

TOMMY
Sure Coach!

He runs back toward the field.

88. MEDIUM GROUP

TOMMY MILLS comes back to center with FRANK and HAGEN.

MILLS
Try centering for awhile Frank.

FRANK
(puzzled)
Sure Coach.

MILLS
(grins at the
others discomfort)
You'll like that position...
Alright you guys, hit the line.

FL - 44

89. WIDE

With KNUTE watching far in the background the men hit the line. FRANK takes center. The play (TO THE DISCRETION OF THE DIRECTOR).

DISSOLVE TO:

90. INT. LONG HALLWAY - LONG - NIGHT

FRANK in his pajamas is practicing his passing by tossing the ball down the long hallway to a matress and a few other back up articles. There is the constant thud as the ball hits then bounces back along the hall toward him to retrieve. Suddenly one of the doors flies open and a sleepy STUDENT comes out into the hall.

STUDENT
Come on Leahy, knock it off.
It's after midnight. Don't
you ever get tired.

ANOTHER STUDENT (o.s.)
Yeah...I got exams tomorrow.

FRANK
Okay...in just a minute.

He lets go of the ball, and the STUDENT goes back into his room in disgust. He slams the door behind him. FRANK retrieves the ball and gives it another hard pass, only this time when the loud thud comes over all the doors open and papers, pillows, etc come flying out at him...It is a mess...then the students themselves show themselves and continue throwing things at him...This continues until....

91. CLOSE FIGURE - FATHER O'DELL

Standing at the clear end of the hall. He clears his throat loudly.

93. LONG - TO THE ACTION

The STUDENTS make a hasty retriet. The doors close quietly behind them....

To the Discretion of the Director part III

We begin to see Wood's limitations writing about sports here as a practice scene is dramatized. To Wood's credit, he actually allows a practice scene to play out on the field rather than having characters discuss it off the field. However, he uses "To the discretion of the Director" twice, both as the scene begins and ends, seemingly as a placeholder for what should be descriptions of football action.

FL - 45

94. MEDIUM CLOSE - FRANK

as FATHER O'DELL comes in to confront him.

FATHER O'DELL
A little distant from the field,
isn't it Frank?

FRANK
Errrr...Hello Father O'Dell.

FATHER O'DELL
Don't you think there might
be more favorable places for
you to practice and at a more
decent hour?

FRANK
Guess you're right, Father...

FATHER O'DELL starts off.

But, how about one for the
road...

FATHER O'DELL
(thinking)
Why not...

FATHER O'DELL starts his run down the hall. He hurdles the mattress and FRANK let's go...

95. MEDIUM CLOSE - FATHER O'DELL

The ball is too high for him and heading for the stained glass window at the end of the hall.

96. CLOSE - FRANK

Shocked...

97. CLOSE - FATHER O'DELL

Looking to the window...a look of horror.

98. MEDIUM

The ball hits the window solidly...It doesn't break... the ball bounces back into the corridor to land at FATHER O'DELL'S feet...He looks down at it.

CONTINUED

FL - 46

98. CONTINUED

FATHER O'DELL clasps his hands and lifts his eyes sky-ward...

FATHER O'DELL
Saint's be praised....

99. CLOSE - FRANK

Lifts his eyes skyward.

FRANK
That goes for the two of us.

FADE TO:

100. INT. CLASSROOM - CLOSE FIGURE - DAY

FAHTER MICHEL is with his French class.

FATHER MICHEL
'Les enfants du soleil jouent
en la pluis.'

101. WIDE

FATHER MICHEL
How would you translate that
sentence, Mr. Leahy?

LEAHY
I'd have to hear it again,
Father.

There is a humorous snicker which the FAHTER glares down. FRANK coughs a couple of times and the FATHER centers his glafe on FRANK.

FATHER MICHEL
Mr. Leahy, I know football is a
time-consuming activity, but
if you don't stop studying it
in this class I most certainly
will be forced to penalize
you, when it comes to semester's
end.

CONTINUED

Hallway Practice

This is a genuinely funny scene that is an amalgamation of two stories from the Williams book, with additional material by Wood thrown in to give it a legitimate punch line.

In the book, the first story about practicing in the hallway has Leahy's classmates complaining and a Father Pete (not O'Dell) coming to tell him to knock it off, but then agreeing to do one last play with him which results in the ball crashing against a students' door.

The second story involves sending a punt pass through a window and the rector coming up to see what's going on. It's unclear if through a window means through an open window, or actually breaking a window.

Wood improves on this by combining these stories, getting comic relief out of Leahy's annoyed dorm neighbors and ending it with the miracle of the unbroken stained glass window, along with the prayer punchline. This is a truly cinematic way to show Leahy practicing, without having to either dramatize an actual football practice, or leave one up to the director's discretion.

French Class

There's no mention of French class or Father Michel in Williams' book, so aside from creating dramatic tension, I'm not sure why Wood conceived of and included this scene.

For the record, "Les enfants du soleil jouent en la pluis" translates to "The children of the sun play in the rain," which strikes me as an odd phrase to be learning. It made me wonder if it was a famous quote from somewhere but a quick Google returned nothing. It sounds like some serious hippie stuff that doesn't seem time appropriate for this story *or* the time in which it was written. Where does Wood come up with this stuff?

FL - 47

101. CONTINUED

FRANK
I'm sorry Father. I just haven't been feeling too well lately. I'm getting a little run down, I guess.

FATHER MICHEL
That is quite apparent.

FRANK coughs again.

And if that cough continues I suggest you check in at the infirmary.

FRANK
I'll do that Father Michel!

A bell rings ending the class. The men begin to gather up their books, notes, etc.

FATHER MICHEL
We'll continue this discussion of French tomorrow, Mr. Leahy. I further suggest that you put in some extra time on your studies so that you will be prepared.

FRANK
I expect so...
(almost under his breath)

FATHER MICHEL
What was that Mr. Leahy?

FRANK
Oh, I said...yes, sir. I'll do that.

The FATHER closes a book on his desk and exits the class room through a rear door.

MULLINS
Frank, you ought to know that he's about the toughst old bird on this campus. I hear tell he'd rather flunk a football player than any-one else. You've got to keep up that seventy-seven average or

CONTINUED

48.

101. CONTINUED

MULLINS (cont'd)
you don't play football at this university.

FRANK
Yeah, I doubt if even the great Knute Rockne with all his pull could influence this guy.

MULLINS
You can bet on that...

102. EXT. PRACTICE FIELD - WIDE - DAY

PLAYERS exercise, (TO THE DISCRETION OF THE DIRECTOR.)

KNUTE ROCKNE can be seen somewhere in the background and it is apparent he is keeping a keen eye on FRANK.

FADE TO:

103. INT. FRANK'S DORM ROOM WIDE - ESTABLISHING - NIGHT

There are two sets of double bunk beds, a couple of desk, with lamps, lamps over the head of each bed, the usual university room of the period. The four men are FRANK, MULLINS, STEVE and another MAN who passes out almost as the scene begins. They are doing push ups and are undoubtedly inebriated. When the 4th MAN topples over and has passed out cold the others roll away from their task laughing drunkenly.

FRANK crawls on all fours to his bottom bunk and flops into it. He looks across toward a pathetic Christmas tree in the back corner of the room.

STEVE salutes him from the floor with a drink.

STEVE
I salute the winner from Winner!

FRANK holds out his mug and MULLINS fills it from an ambur bottle.

MULLINS
My buddie, my partner, my team-mate. A winner all the way.

CONTINUED

FL - 49

103. CONTINUED

FRANK
(drinks - coughs)
Where'd you get this rot-gut.

MULLINS
From my brother...'comes all the way from St. Louis.

FRANK
That I can believe. Thought the stuff tasted like it came from the stockyards...Ah...

STEVE
(bleary)
Hell of a Christmas this is.

FRANK
There's snow on the ground. Besides Christmas is still a week off and both of you...
(indicates man on the floor)
and him will be spread all over the country by then.

STEVE
Why didn't you take your brother up on his offer of dough to see that you got home for the holidays?

FRANK
Ah...
(waves his hand then drinks and makes a face)
As much as I already drank of this stuff tonight you'd think I'd be gettin' used to it by this time. Ugh..this is really foul...
(pace change)
Gene's a great guy. We're gonna' do some pro ball this summer.

MULLINS
(horrified)
You can't do that. You can't play pro and University.

CONTINUED

FL - 50

103. CONTINUED

FRANK
(waving him off)
Ahhh, not football, baseball.
He's got a wife and kids, Gene
that is. I can't take money
from him....
(winks)
You know what? He was so
proud of me going to Notre
Dame he was going to help
finance me all the way!
I couldn't let him do that
either.

STEVE
(rolls over on
the floor onto
his stomach)
Your folks not too well off?

FRANK
Naw! They're fixed alright.
Nice farm and everything...
But that's a long story.

STEVE
Okay, so while we're away you
can care-take the place for us.

FRANK
I'll miss your ugly pusses, but
it'll be nice to have the place
to myself for a change...I can
use the peace and quiet...

MULLINS
Peace and quiet??? You? With
your push-ups and the grunts that
accompany them...sprinting and
passing and shoving the line down
the halls... Peace and quiet!
Well for the next couple of weeks
you can do the whole routine
all you want...to your hearts
content, but knowing your heart...
it's never content.

The MAN on the floor groans, rolls over then comes to almost a sitting position, but then sinks to the floor again with a deep moan....

CONTINUED

FL - 51

103. CONTINUED

FRANK
Is he out again.

STEVE leans over the man, then rights himself again.

STEVE
Co....cold....Look. This grog has made me hungry. The kitchen is still well stocked. Maybe most of the students have already left but the Padres still have to eat.

FRANK
The kitchen is locked.

MULLINS
(winks)
We have ways...Come on...

The three men stagger to their feet.

WIPE DISSOLVE

104. INT. THE KITCHEN - MEDIUM - NIGHT

The only light in the massive kitchen is from the crack of the walk-in refrigeration system. The boys are finishing their gigantic snack when MULLINS gets an idea. His eyes lighten up and he snaps his fingers. He jumps to his feet and races back into the refrigerator and is gone from the scene for a long moment. The others stare after him, in wonderment. MULLINS returns carrying a chicken by the neck.

STEVE
What's that for?

MULLINS
Ever hear of a chicken - hawk?

FRANK
I don't get him...do you?

MULLINS
You're not supposed to get me... you're supposed to follow me... Come on....

He leads the way out of the kitchen. FRANK holds back only long enough to slam the refrigerator door. MULLINS has picked up a can of cooking oil and shoves it to STEVE.

Dorm Drinking

No sequence analogous to this appears in Williams' book; however, Mullins being one of Leahy's roommates is accurate to the book, and the fact that it was four men to a room is also accurate. This sequence serves to set up another comedic sequence that is not in the Williams book, and a couple things are briefly mentioned in dialogue that set up later scenes, but other than that it's hard to understand exactly what this scene adds to the Leahy story. Drinking was important to Wood, and a major part of his life by the time he was writing this screenplay, so it's a possibility it was simply on his mind.

Was Wood writing from personal experience? Did he ever sit around a dorm room drinking with his roommates while doing pushups? It seems like a strangely specific setup to come right off the top of his head, but it's also unclear if he ever went to college. There are a couple sources that put him in some kind of higher education in the tiny window after his military service and before he got to Hollywood, but nothing is certain. Although, speaking of Wood's military service, sitting around drinking and doing pushups seems like something a bunch of Marines might do, so maybe he's dipping into that experience.

The bit of storytelling here about Gene offering to help pay for Leahy's college is needlessly confusing and a classic example of a bit of information that seems conspicuous if only because it hasn't already been mentioned. There were already entire scenes in this screenplay devoted to where Leahy's going to get the money to go to college, wouldn't Gene's offer have been something worth bringing up then? Also, as mentioned before, if Leahy's got a scholarship, what's he need money for? It's all needlessly confusing and convoluted. Incidentally, in the book, Leahy says his brother *did* help him with money at Notre Dame.

The mention of playing pro baseball over the summer is actually a rare setup for something that does actually happen later in the screenplay, though it's only mentioned in passing in the book.

FL - 52

105. EXT. CAMPUS - WASHINGTON HALL - ANGLED - NIGHT

The campus is quiet, as three dark shadows creep across to the mascot HAWK...They tear it from it's perch and replace it with the chicken. Then with the CAMERA PANNING, they move to enter the building.

106. INT. HALL - LONG SHOT - NIGHT

The hall is dimly lighted but the highly polished floor shines brightly. The first thing they do is to spread the oil from wall to wall and make the spread about three feet wide. FRANK is on the opposite side of the puddle and they all laugh lightly, drunkenly.

The job finally done MULLINS looks to FRANK.

MULLINS
You know what to do.

FRANK
Now?

MULLINS
No time like the present.

The two boys watch as FRANK goes to the fire alarm and pulls it...a hell of a racket breaks loose and as the men, in various stages of undress, push open their doors and start to stream out. FRANK runs and jumps the grease, but hits the very edge of it with his heel. He goes down on his rump and twists his knee in the process...But he makes it to his feet and hobble-runs after MULLINS and STEVE.

The Washington Hall boys are racing for the front exit some chasing those who are fleeing and others simply running because they still believe there is a fire.

Just before they reach the puddle MULLINS turns and tosses the HAWK at their feet. They are coming too fast to stop and they hit the grease...the pile up is a head over tail mass of arms, legs and heads becoming a giant snake pit.

FADE TO:

Impractical Jokers

So, a scene that wasn't in the book set up this sequence, which is also not in the book. Aside from maybe being an example of what Wood misguidedly considers "typical college fun," it's hard to imagine what purpose this sequence is supposed to serve in the story of Leahy's life.

Oddly enough, for Wood, this sequence is set up in passing earlier in the screenplay on page 38 when Leahy asks Mullins about the building with the stuffed hawk in front of it. Mullins says this is Washington Hall, where the upper classmen live, and that the stuffed hawk is the hall's mascot. So, in this prank sequence, Leahy and the boys replace the stuffed hawk with a dead chicken from the kitchen, lube up the floors of the hall with cooking oil, and pull the fire alarm.

There is a Washington Hall on Notre Dame's campus, but it's a venue for events, meetings, lectures, performances and rehearsals – not a residence hall. As far as I can tell, it has served this function since the 1880s and I couldn't find any references to the building having a stuffed hawk as a mascot. So either Wood made all this stuff up, or he was misinformed. If he made it up, it seems odd that he'd include well-researched details on one page, then make something up out of whole cloth on the next – it's not as if there aren't probably many strange Notre Dame traditions Wood could have pulled from.

In any case, this prank sequence goes out with a whimper and has no bearing on anything that comes next. We do cut to Rockne lecturing the boys directly after this, but it's a totally unrelated lecture, not a "Stop goofing off" lecture. So, Leahy cries wolf, once again, this time by pulling a fire alarm, and gets off scot-free.

FL - 53

107. INT. RECREATION ALL - CLOSE FIGURE - KNUTE - DAY

KNUTE is facing his off scene men...

KNUTE
Well boys, it's been a great football season, but it's all over now, and it's up to you fellows to get in there and double up on your time in classes when you get back from the holidays so you can pass your examinations...

108. MEDIUM - PAN

The CAMERA pans the faces of them men, mainly the front row is seen but the other rows behind them are seen in passing also. FRANK, and MULLINS are in the front row and it is apparent they are suffering monumental hand-overs. KNUTE'S voice comes over the shot.

KNUTE (o.s.)
Many of you will be here for spring football which there's been some objection to, and I also object myself because I can see your side...where it interferes with your drinking and courting the skirts...

FRANK and MULLINS both have winced at the mention of drinking. The others only nervously laugh.

109. WIDE - SIDE VIEW

of KNUTE ROCKNE and his men.

KNUTE
But you damn well hear this. When you're home with your family and friends you can eat all the candy canes and mince pie ala modes you want, but if there's a single ounce of fat on you next spring I'll scratch your name from the roster. And if you're looking to line up a job for next summer, remember how much I hate 'mezzanine cowboys' athletes

CONTINUED

Mezzanine Cowboys

Another colorful speech for whoever would have had the pleasure of playing Knute Rockne. In case you're wondering, a quick Google for the expression "mezzanine cowboys" came up empty, so I think maybe Wood's coined a phrase here. Seems like it'd make a good movie title, like *Reservoir Dogs*.

FL - 54

109. CONTINUED

KNUTE (cont'd)
who take it easy sortin' mail or jockeyin' a desk. So Merry Christmas, Happy New Year and thank you for a great season... next year will be even better.

110. CLOSE - FIGURE - ROCKNE

He reaches to a stand near him and picks up the Hering Award.

KNUTE
And now for the presentation of the Hering Awards, given to those players, Varsity abd Freshmen, judged most proficient in their respective positions.

SCREEN WIPE TO:

111. MEDIUM - ANGLED

ANGLED across FRANK to KNUTE. MOON MULLINS has just has just received his award and shakes KNUTE'S hand and leaves the front position. KNUTE looks in FRANK'S direction. The others applause and when the applause dies...

KNUTE
And last but far from least... for outstanding play at center, Freshman Frank Leahy...

FRANK is momentarily spellbound, but manages to get to his feet. He goes to the beaming KNUTE who hands him the medal.

KNUTE
Congratulations Frank.

FRANK
(awed)
Thanks Coach...thanks so much.

FADE TO:

Hering (sic) Awards

In Williams' book, Leahy explains a South Bend man, Frank Herring (not Hering), paid $500 a year to supply ten medals at the end of every football season, to be awarded to the best athletes on the team.

It's worth noting Wood's typing seems to go off the deep end here, as he gets Herring's name wrong, spells "and" incorrectly and capitalizes "Freshman" before deciding to lowercase it and go back to strike out the capital F, all within a few keystrokes of each other.

FL - ■ - 55

112. EXT. ROCK QUARRY MEDIUM CLOSE - HOT SUMMER DAY

FRANK is swinging a heavy sledge hammer, breaking the rocks. His body is dirty and rivered with sweat but his body seems more muscular and firmer than it has ever been before. We can't say that he is enjoying the work, but in the true Leahy spirit he is doing the job to the best of his ability and that's the very best. A WHISTLE blows. FRANK has had the hammer poised for another blow. He does not throw it. Instead he lowers it easily and permits the instrument to rest up against a large rock while he takes a handkerchief from his pocket, wipes his brow, replaces the handkerchief then picks up the hammer again and slings it over his shoulder. He walks out of the scene.

113. WIDE

FRANK, along with several other men move to a truck of the period and deposit their instruments then gather around the FOREMAN, near the truck, who is handing out the pay checks. FRANK is the last to receive his.

114. CLOSE TWO - FRANK & FOREMAN

FOREMAN
You're one of the best damned workers I've ever had Leahy.

FRANK
Thanks...<u>coach</u>.

The man laughs.

FOREMAN
I used a fireman once who was on vacation...he used to call me chief.

FRANK
I guess most of us fall into a pattern.

FOREMAN
Yeah, guess that's a fact alright. You comin' back Monday?

FRANK
Two more Mondays. Two more weeks to the summer vacation.

CONTINUED

FL - 56

114. CONTINUED

FOREMAN
You and your brother playing ball
over at the field this weekend?

FRANK
Sure. No rest for the wicked.

FOREMAN
(shakes head)
Say...when do you find time for
any fun?

FRANK
Oh, I guess I just look around
sometimes and there it is...

FOREMAN
(laughs)
Okay...here, take your check.

The FOREMAN hands FRANK the check. FRANK glances at it, folds it and puts it into his pocket.

Come on. Hop into the truck and
I'll give you a lift back to town.

115. WIDE

To complete the action. FRANK and the FOREMAN get into the cab of the truck. The other men are boarding a bus of the period. The vehicles drive off.

DISSOLVE TO:

116. EXT. BASEBALL FIELD - WIDE - ESTABLISHING - DAY

A BASEBALL game is in progress, (TO THE DISCRETION OF THE DIRECTOR.) A homerun is hit and the small town crowd goes wild....The game is over.

117. CLOSE TWO - FRANK & GENE

They are leaving the field with their arms around each other's shoulders...Suddenly FRANK'S eyes catch some-thing of interest off scene...

CONTINUED

Quarry

In Williams' book, Leahy's summer jobs are mentioned in passing, explaining in one sentence that he'd do manual labor in the morning and baseball practice in the afternoon, hauling stuff (including crushed rock) from the railroad depot to the stores. Wood transforms this into almost two full pages detailing Leahy's job at a rock quarry, going into great detail explaining his actions and including some fun dialogue with his foreman. Putting myself in Wood's shoes, I can only imagine he was luxuriating in anything that wasn't sports related any chance he got, but you have to wonder, from a practical standpoint, how much precious real estate is wasted in this script, taken up with stuff that's totally ancillary to the point of the story.

There is one line I particularly like, though. It stands out as particularly well written, for Wood, and might be my favorite line in the whole screenplay. When the foreman asks Leahy when he has time for fun, Leahy has a response worthy of the likes of Raymond Chandler or Charles Bukowski: "Oh, I guess I just look around sometimes and there it is…"

To the Discretion of the Director part IV

Faced with the prospect of describing a baseball game, Wood decides to leave it up to the director. Also, in case you're keeping score, we've now seen Leahy box and play in a baseball game, but we've yet to see him play in a football game – almost an hour into a movie that is ostensibly about his football career. Yes, he's thrown a shoe and we saw him practice, but come on.

FL - 57

117. CONTINUED

FRANK stops his forward movement which causes GENE TO stop also. FRANK does not remove his eyes from off scene.

FRANK
Hold it.

GENE looks to him, and to where he is looking.

118. MEDIUM CLOSE - HENNY

HENNY a lovely auburn-haired girl, seated near the bottom of the bleechers. She is looking directly at FRANK and she has a <u>come</u>-<u>on</u> glint to her eyes, a warm inviting smile.

119. CLOSE TWO - FRANK & GENE

GENE grins broadly. FRANK pats him on the shoulder.

GENE
See what you mean.

FRANK
I'll catch up with you later.

GENE
Like tomorrow at game time!

FRANK
Something like that.

120. ANGLED - MEDIUM

To take in the girl in the background as FRANK walks away from GENE, and GENE walks toward the players bench to gather up his things. Other players and fans are leaving the field. FRANK goes to the girl and puts his foot up on the bleechers next to her, leans his elbows on the upraised knee. He talks to her for several seconds (<u>unheard</u> <u>on</u> <u>the</u> <u>sound</u> <u>track</u>) then he helps her down to ground level. She takes his arm and they start off.

WIPE DISSOLVE TO:

Henny

Henny is a character completely created by Wood and the following sequence starring her is not in the Williams book at all.

Williams does touch on Leahy's ways with women a couple times in his book, however; first to say, "his good looks had endowed him with captivating, magnetic powers on women. He truly had female adoration." And later, "He was a fine dresser because he was a good ladies' man. He knew women and the psychological thinking behind their motives. He collected women. They were his prime hobby. He judged them before they judged him. As an escort for the female, he was better company than the most fabulous of king's jesters."

There's also an illustration near the back of the book of Leahy, coaching from the sidelines, becoming distracted by a couple cheerleaders (as one of his athletes attempts to hide his erection).

Why the name Henny? It's not a particularly common name. These days, people refer to Hennessy cognac as "Henny" so it's possible Wood used alcohol as an inspiration here, though it's unclear how far back the slang term "Henny" goes. It appeared in popular music starting in the 90s, but did people use the term back in the 70s? Even if they did, I've never seen cognac listed as one of Wood's go-to drinks, so this entire paragraph is probably a stretch.

Wood seemed enamored of names that could be both masculine and feminine, or that had masculine and feminine forms. The most obvious example is the title character Glen in *Glen or Glenda*, who becomes Glenda when he dresses in women's clothing, but the device recurs with many names throughout his writing. Obscure as it is, Henny is a name given to both men and women, and is sometimes the shortened version of Henrietta, the feminine version of Henry.

FL - 58

121. INT. THEATRE - CLOSE TWO - FRANK & HENNY - D/N

FRANK and HENNY are reflected in the darkness by the flickering light from the screen. The music issuing is from the "JAZZ SINGER". But FRANK and HENNY are paying, at this point, no attention to the screen. They are locked into a deep embrace, a heated one which will lead to an affair under any other circumstances except that which will happen.

AL JOLSON (o.s.)
You ain't heard nothin' yet!

FRANK's hands snap away from the girl. He bolts up right in his chair, frantically looks all around him as a little boy caught in the cookie jar. Then he looks to the screen where the song "MAMMY" has begun.

122. FOTTAGE - MAMMY

Showing a portion of Jolson singing "Mammy" (IF POSSIBLE, & AVAILABLE).

123. CLOSE TWO - FRANK & HENNY

She is extremely heated, wanting more of what FRANK has been giving her. She claws at him trying to get him back. Her hands try everything in that direction. She is almost in tears from her sexual demands.

HENNY
Frank...oh Frank, Frank, Frank.

FRANK
Look Henny, look...at the screen.
(points.)

HENNY
I know, I know, I know...I've seen it before...Ohhh, come on Frank, be nice to me...Oh I need you, what you can do for me...Oh, what you do to me.

FRANK
He's talking...singing...I mean look...right up there on the screen....

CONTINUED

FL - 59

123. CONTINUED

He is leaning completely forward now with his hands on the back of the seat in front of him. The trembling girl is completely neglected.

It is at this point that a handsome young man just behind her leans forward and taps her lightly on the shoulder. She quickly looks to him. He whispers his words to her but he might just as well have shouted because FRANK is completely engrossed in voices from the screen.

YOUNG MAN

I'm available!

HENNY glances to FRANK then back to the young MAN...

HENNY

So am I...

She gets up and she and the young man leave the scene in the direction of the front exit. FRAMK is oblivious of what has happened.

124. INT. SPEECH CLASS - MEDIUM FIGURE - PULL BACK TO WIDE - DAY

FRANK is in the middle of his speech, one about what he did with his summer. Behind him is a board denoting that this is SPEECH CLASS 201 and the teacher is FATHER DONELLY.

FRANK

(obviously nervous)

Then came the big shocker...the voice jumps at you right out from the screen...

The CAMERA BEGINS A SLOW PULL BACK TOWARD THE WIDE ANGLE to take in the entire class room.

Well not you can sum up everything you see that comes along new in life, but this takes the cake. I don't see how anything is ever going to beat that...voices right there with the moving pictures. Then I came back to school a couple of days early and worked out with the new equipment and

CONTINUED

The Jazz Singer

Although Leahy notes his love of the movies a couple times in Williams' book, this specific sequence is completely fabricated by Wood. It is interesting for multiple reasons. The first is that it brings one of Wood's greatest loves, movies, into the action. This becomes a repeating motif, as movies tend to show up as important moments occur, later in the screenplay. Note how Wood lovingly describes Leahy and Henny "reflected in the darkness by the flickering light from the screen." This short description sets the mood better than many of Wood's longer descriptions, perhaps because the atmosphere of a movie theater was holy in his mind.

The second point of interest in this sequence is the sexed-up dialogue from Henny. In the last decade of his life, when this screenplay was written, Wood also wrote and directed pornographic loops, most notably in the Swedish Erotica line. These loops were silent, but featured inter-titles written by Wood so viewers didn't miss super important stuff, like what the actors and actresses were saying, and often what sounds they might be making.

Henny's dialogue here is written much as the loop inter-titles Wood was used to writing, and also bears some similarity to the dialogue in the countless sex novels Wood churned out in the 60s and 70s. The repetition, the ellipses and the over-the-top arousal of Henny are all classic Wood hallmarks.

This scene is also buttoned up nicely at the end, with a quick joke about Henny moving on to another man sitting nearby when she fails to get Leahy's attention back from Al Jolson. Some sources say 1931's *Dracula* with Wood's future friend, Bela Lugosi, was the first film Wood ever saw, so if that's true, Leahy's fascination with the advent of sound cinema isn't directly from Wood's personal experience. But, the sheer awe of movie magic most certainly was.

FL - 60

124. CONTINUED

FRANK (cont'd)
that's how I spent my summer
vacation..."The End."

The class laugh, and FATHER DONELLY grins broadly.

FATHER DONELLY
That was very nice Mr. Leahy...
You will do very well in speech,
and I do think that one day you
could make quite an after dinner
speaker...but you really don't
have to say, "The End" at the
end of your speech...No...No...
No...that just isn't done.

The class really laughs it up...

WIPE DISSOLVE TO:

125. EXT. PRACTICE FIELD - EXTREME CLOSE HEAD - ROCKNE - DAY

KNUTE ROCKNE'S head fills the screen.

KNUTE
Okay boys...this is the start
of a new year...and it's going
to be the greatest year yet...

The CAMERA PULLS back swiftly to show the entire scene. ROCKNE'S players and the crew of an antiquated camera and sound equipment and their truck with "R.C.A. PHOTOPHONE" printed on the side....

DIRECTOR
CUT!!!

The DIRECTOR gets out of his chair and crosses to KNUTE.

We got to put more life in it
Coach...I mean zest...people
expect you coaches to be tough,
and with all this new sound,
they want to hear "TOUGH".
Can't let the fans down the first
time they can actually hear you
talking to your players...

CONTINUED

The End

This scene represents a rare moment in the screenplay, perhaps the only one so far, in which something Leahy experiences leads directly to the results of the next scene. Most screenplays are full of cause and effect and character growth. In this one it's sparing. Here, Leahy's amazement at seeing his first sound film translates directly into him giving a good speech in class, which is perhaps a little foreshadowing for his upcoming public speaking career. This little bit about saying "the end" at the end of a speech isn't in the book, so I wonder if Wood ever had this taught to him and is remembering it here.

FL - 61

125. CONTINUED

KNUTE
Hell fella, I'm a football coach, not one of your Hollywood actors.

DIRECTOR
And that's just what we want you to be...yourself...Now we'll do it again...be yourself...be yourself...

The DIRECTOR walks back to his chair and sits down...

126. CLOSE TWO - KNUTE & FRANK

KNUTE winks at FRANK who gets what he means with a nod of his head.

127. CLOSE - DIRECTOR

Preparing....

DIRECTOR
Ready coach?

KNUTE (o.s.)
When ever you are.

DIRECTOR
Camera...

CAMERAMAN (o.s.)
Camera rolling...

DIRECTOR
Sound...

SOUNDMAN (o.s.)
...Speed...

DIRECTOR
Alright, coach....action...

128. CLOSE - KNUTE ROCKNE - FIGURE

He forms his most ferocious glare, and digs his feet wide apart and smashes his doubled up fists into his hips as he faces his men...directly toward CAMERA.

CONTINUED

FL - 62

128. CONTINUED

KNUTE
(fierce)
Alright, you sons-a-bitches, yer back, and by damned yer gonna run yer asses off up and down that....

129. CLOSE - DIRECTOR

In a state of complete shock...

KNUTE (o.s.)
...field until yer dim-witted bastard brains....

130. MEDIUM - FEATURING KNUTE

Moving heavily around the players.

KNUTE
think they're rotting in hell... And then for good measure I'm gonna' kick hell outta' ever mother's son....

131. MEDIUM - CAMERA CREW

All in shock, startled amazement...The DIRECTOR flies out of his chair waving his arms and screaming his words...

DIRECTOR
CUT...CUT...CUT...

He falls back into his chair in pure exasperation.

We'll...We'll finish this after lunch!!! Somebody get me a tranquiler....

132. WIDE

The entire team is doubled up in laughter...KNUTE puts his arm around FRANK'S shoulder and still laughing they walk off along the field.

FL - 63

133. MEDIUM TWO - MOVING - FRANK & KNUTE

The CAMERA TRUCKS with KNUTE and FRANK.

ROCKNE
That outta' set sound back twenty-five years...

FRANK
You sure told them what for.

They stop as a PRIEST approaches them.

FATHER
(to a little boy who has played a prank)
Knute...Now do you think that was a nice thing to do to the poor fellow!!!

KNUTE
(grin)
Well, Padre...That's one performance they'll remember all their lives.

The PRIEST slaps KNUTE on the back and goes off laughing. FRANK and KNUTE continue their walk along the field.

KNUTE
Frank...You know the varsity team is leaving for Wisconsin this Friday, don't you?

FRANK
(down-cast)
Who doesn't?

CONTINUED

More Movies

Another movie-related scene quickly follows the last one, this time presenting movie magic from the production side in another seeming cause and effect scene, implying Leahy's interest in sound films has led directly to the production of a movie about Knute Rockne and his team. This is another sequence that has no match in the book. It seems every time this screenplay goes to the movies, it's pure Wood.

Curious if this sequence could be matched up with a real movie, I did a little research and dug up some sound footage of Rockne coaching his players circa 1929 for a Fox Movietone News story called *Fighting Irish Are Turned Loose*. There's no extreme close up of Rockne's face, as the screenplay has it, but he does bark orders at the team before the short film moves on to show the team practicing. I don't know if Wood was aware of this film, which now resides at the University of South Carolina, but 1929 is the exact time this scene would have taken place, being the beginning of Leahy's second year at Notre Dame. The University also has silent outtakes from a 1920 Fox Movietone News story, also about Rockne and Notre Dame, that does feature an extreme close up of Rockne – but no sound.

The credits listed on the University of South Carolina's website do not include a director, but list the camera operator as William Storz. There's a real possibility a news reel like this wouldn't have a traditional director, so we can speculate that the "director" character in Wood's screenplay is either meant to be Storz himself, or just a made up character. Either way it is tempting to picture Wood himself stepping in for his cameo as the director. Wood was a naturally talented actor who appeared in many of his own productions, and also some films made by his cronies. By 1975 some might say Wood was in no condition to appear on screen, but he was great in his last confirmed appearance, only a year earlier in 1974's *Fugitive Girls*, and this part would have been perfect for him. He even gives "himself" a memorable last line.

It's rare that Wood's attempts at intentional humor land in his films, so it's notable that so far this screenplay has already had more successful comedic scenes than unsuccessful ones, with Rockne's profanity-laden tirade being probably my favorite.

FL - 64

132. CONTINUED

KNUTE
(starts low and
builds hard)
I don't know what you were playing out there today, but it sure as hell wasn't football.

INTERCUTS of the PLAYERS are thoroughly spaced during KNUTES tirad. Their reactions.

KNUTE
By God. There are dumb players and there are dumber players. You characters follow in the third category. It appears that the only qualifications necessary for holding the position of lineman is to be big and stupid...
...And to be a BACK you only have to be stupid!
Jeff. You should have shown them your scrapbooks. Perhaps they wouldn't have been so tough on you if they knew how good you are...

133. CLOSE - A PLAYER, JEFF.

He is angry at being singled out.

JEFF
I did the best I could!

134. CLOSE - KNUTE

Just as angry he spins on the man again.

ROCKNE
If that's your best I'd hate to see your worst!!!
(fairly screaming)

135. WIDE - THE SCENE.

JEFF
Count me off the team. I'll never play for you again.

CONTINUED

FL - 65.

135. CONTINUED

KNUTE
(spits his words)
You never have!!!

He directs his further words to the entire group.

KNUTE
I coach football to win...and by God you're going to play to win...

136. CLOSE - FRANK

Intense...listening carefully.

EFFECTS DISSOLVE TO

137.---INT. KNUTE ROCKNE'S OFFICE - CLOSE TO FULL - DAY

At the outset we are on FRANK much as the previous scene for the EFFECTS DISSOLVE. (When the scene is in full we will see that ROCKNE'S office is simple, but all of his awards and photos, books and diagrams etc., are in evidence.)

FRANK
I don't think you have much to worry about coach. You love Notre Dame and she loves you.

The CAMERA starts the PULL BACK, SLOWLY, during FRANK'S dialogue and as KNUTE begins his dialogue he is in the shot.

KNUTE
You're only as good as your last few games Frank...always remember that. A looser is soon forgotten. We're saddled with this Army game soon and that means the entire press fire will be there. The New York press has been after my guts for a long time and a loss there would give them just the knife to cut me open...a win...it could be the game of my career.

CONTINUED

Raising the Steaks

Leahy gets his first chance at a road game and the line about dining car steaks is straight out of Williams' book. The book doesn't go into the depressing train ride home from the game that's in the screenplay, which Notre Dame apparently loses, triggering an admonishing speech from Rockne that seems to result in at least one team member quitting right then and there. Wood attempts to raise the stakes by inserting the concept of loss into a movie that has heretofore been all about winning. It's really Leahy's first setback.

It's worth noting that again, Wood builds up to the excitement of a sporting event but then cuts way from it, skipping directly to the train ride home. If he really wanted to portray the sting of defeat and raise the stakes, he could have written an in-game sequence, depicting some of the mistakes the team made on their way to their loss, maybe even involving Leahy directly so he has some personal responsibility. Instead, we continue our football-less football movie in which people discuss games we never get to see.

Nice Dissolve

Moments like the dissolve here, where a close up of Leahy on the train dissolves to a close up of him in Rockne's office, signal that for all his faults, Wood was thinking visually and cinematically as he wrote. Certain parts of the screenplay do go on autopilot, and we have long sections of telling without showing, but every now and then we see a glimmer like this dissolve that Wood actually is picturing a film in his head as he writes.

FL - 66

137. CONTINUED

KNUTE (cont'd)
Which brings me to the reason
I asked you over here. With
Ransavage injured I need a
new backup man for Miller, a
damned good man. I'm switching
you back to tackle...

FRANK is a bit confused.

I know you've put a lot of study
and practice with your center
work, and you're damned good at
it. But I also count on your
determination when it comes to
new challenges thrown at you.
You're a lot like me. You like
to win. I need more men around
me like you...men who thrive on
winning....

FRANK grins, but still is confused....

FADE TO:

138. EXT. CHURCH - WIDE - ESTABLISHING - MORNING

A somber organ is heard from within the church.

139. INT. CHURCH - ANGLED - DAY

The organ is heard over the scene, low...somber. Most or all of the PLAYERS are there but we feature KNUTE, FRANK and MULLINS...A PRIEST moves into the scene and lights a single candle. All the others are kneeling.

140. CLOSE - KNUTE - KNEELING

He cocks his head slightly and watches the PRIEST o.s.

141. CLOSE - PRIEST

He finishes lighting the single candle and turns away.

FL - 67

142. MEDIUM

The PRIEST is about to pass KNUTE who stops him.

KNUTE
A single candle? What's that for?

PRIEST
(grin)
That's lighted for your victory against Army today. And let's pray that GOD'S ARMY has the stronger team.

KNUTE
(eyes candle)
Then don't be so cheap with the wax, Father....

DISSOLVE TO:

143. INT. LOCKER ROOM - WIDE - ESTABLISHING - DAY

The NOTRE DAME team is tired, dirty from the long first half. For the moment it appears they feel they can't go on...it's all over...their spirit is beat....

144. CLOSE - ENTRANCE - ROCKNE

KNUTE frames himself in the doorway. He senses the attitude and if he had a pep talk scheduled he drops it and changes his approach. He becomes all cheer.

145. WIDE - THE SCENE

ROCKNE
Don't worry boys, we'll touchdown before they do. There's still half a game to be played.

JERRY
(limp)
Coach they've got <u>us</u> pooped and <u>they</u> haven't even begun to play yet.

CONTINUED

Don't Be So Cheap with the Wax, Father

Another genuinely funny moment between Rockne and a priest, as the priest lights a single candle for Notre Dame's victory and Rockne has the great punch line, "Then don't be so cheap with the wax, Father…" a quote not found in the pages of Williams' book.

A lot of the funniest moments in this screenplay are interactions with men of the cloth, so Wood obviously got a kick out of juxtaposing the solemnity of religious tradition with the no-nonsense approach of your average Joe.

This kind of back and forth also continues to position Rockne as a suitably memorable character, as he starts to steal the movie as perhaps the only guy with personality in the cast list.

FL - 68

145. CONTINUED

KNUTE
Neither have we...Neither have we!

He makes a pace change and becomes dead serious for his pep talk.

INTERCUTS of the players will be used throughout KNUTE'S pep talk and we will see the PLAYERS changing attitudes to a winning team.

KNUTE
I've got a story to tell you. It's a sad story, but it's also a winning story. I had something else I was going to pep you up with. But right now I think what I've got to say is more appropriate...

He pauses and surveys his men to make sure he has all of their attentions...hehas.

KNUTE
None of you personally knew George Gipp, but you've all heard about him. Now teams ain't supposed to go by the star system...to have a single star. But The Gipp was Notre Dame's brightest star. When he didn't play the crowds went wild, screamed for him..."We want Gipp...We want Gipp!!"
We had one particularly cold day that one particular game. Gipp was warming the seat of his pants on the bench because he had a particularly bad cold. None of us knew just how bad that cold was. Gipp wasn't one to complain or see doctors if he could get out of it. Well anyway. The crowds looked like they might tear out the bleechers when they started shouting, "We want Gipp...We want Gipp". Gipp thrived on that kind of action, and he pleaded with me to send him in. I did! I sent him in!
(he brings tears to his eyes)

CONTINUED

FL - 69

145. CONTINUED

KNUTE (cont'd)
A few days later he was dead!
But....
(pace change)
...but, before he died he said to me. "Rock. Sometime when the team is up against it, when the breaks are going all against you, tell them to go in there and win one for the Gipper. I'll be watching from my vantage point, and when they do win, I'll be the happiest man in heaven."
So let's get out there AND WIN ONE FOR THE GIPPER!!!

The team tears loose with enthusiasm...FRANK joins several of the others who have stood up and started applauding.

146. INT. PRESS ROOM - GROUP - DAY

ANGLED FEATURING KNUTE ROCKNE as he talks to the press

KNUTE
And you can put this in your paper. Sure we beat Army, but it's been just about the worst year football has ever had, and that's all football, all the teams and all the coaches...a lot of mistakes have been made... but that's not stopping any of us. We've got to find the weaknesses and make changes... resolve to do better next year. That's the good old American way and there's nothing more American than Mother, Apple Pie and Foot-ball....

FADE TO:

147. INT. TERRI'S APARTMENT - MEDIUM SHOT - NIGHT

Only the lights of the city come through the window and there are the dark shadows of a lovely blonde

CONTINUED

Knute Rockne All American

After suitable buildup to an important game, Wood cuts directly to the locker room at halftime. This lack of football and complete avoidance of in-game action is beginning to verge on parody.

The Rockne speech given here, about George Gipp's last words, is the famous speech he gave in the locker room at Yankee Stadium after the first half of Notre Dame's November 10th, 1928 game against Army. It is also dramatized at the climax of *Knute Rockne All American*. Wood doesn't replicate it word for word, but it's close enough.

This is a difficult position for a screenwriter to be in. The phrase "Win one for the Gipper" had already long since taken on a life of its own by this point, and the scenes covered in this sequence of the screenplay had already been famously covered in a well received and remembered film. At the same time, Wood must have felt like he couldn't simply skip over it, since it would have been an important moment in Leahy's life, and is even called out as such in Williams' biography. So, he seemingly had no choice in this thankless task, other than to attempt to tell the story without completely cribbing another movie.

Of course, in Wood's world, what you do after this rousing speech is cut directly to the post game press conference. In *Knute Rockne All American*, the action cuts to the football field, where we witness Notre Dame's triumphant first touchdown against Army, as a proud Rockne watches from the sidelines. I'll leave it up to you which seems more dramatically satisfying.

FL - 70

147. CONTINUED

and FRANK. This is TERRI an actress of sorts. She might or might not have done what she says.

TERRI
You're insatiable, Frank. Are all footballers like that?

FRANK
They talk a lot...but I've never been in the bedroom with them to see first hand.

TERRI
Oh, you....
(giggles)

FRANK
You really been in the follies, Terri?

TERRI
Sure. Want to see my press notices?

FRANK
I'll take your word for it.

TERRI
I've played New York, Los Angeles, Chicago, San Francisco...Have you been to those places?

FRANK
I will someday. But I go to the movies a lot and I guess I know what they look like.

TERRI
There is nothing like being on my side of the footlights. All the glamour and the glory of it...But I guess you guess you get glamour and glory being a football hero too, don't you? All the girls chasing you. Do you have a lot of girls chasing you Frank?

CONTINUED

Terri

There is no "Terri" character in Williams' book, but it's a typically Woodian move to skip over football scenes that are important to the plot while inserting a sex scene that does nothing to move the story forward.

In a derisive side note, Wood makes sure to mention Terri is an actress "of sorts." A few lines later we learn she performed in "the follies" and has played big cities all over the country. The lack of capitalization on "follies" suggests she is not referencing the Ziegfeld Follies. The follies Wood would have had firsthand experience with would have been The Follies Theater, a burlesque house in Los Angeles, the performers of which crossed over into many George Weiss-produced films for Quality Studios – the man who produced *Glen or Glenda* and the studio in which it was shot.

A "Terri" character appears in Wood's short story *Like a Hole in the Head.* It appeared in the November/December 1971 issue of *Pendulum* vol. 3, no. 1, a pornographic magazine published by Wood's on-and-off employer, Bernie Bloom. The Terri in that story is also an actress "of sorts", with a plan to seduce her way to stardom.

By the time Wood wrote this screenplay, the majority of his work for years had been in the adult industry, so a scene like this must have come as second nature to him. Indeed, the "banter" would fit right into one of the many sexploitation screenplays he wrote for Stephen Apostolof.

I would be remiss if I did not point out that Terri is a name that can be used for both women and men… Terri/Terry or Terri/Terrance.

By the way, it's funny to imagine the framing device we started with when we land in a scene like this – are we to believe Bernie Williams is regaling his little son with tales of Leahy's sexual conquests?

FL - 71

147. CONTINUED

FRANK
I get my share....
(after thought)
And then some...

TERRI
As pretty as me?

FRANK
That's a silly question.

TERRI
Why is it silly?

FRANK
An actress has to be the prettiest of all or she wouldn't be an actress now would she?

TERRI
That's a pretty thing to say.

FRANK
Well, it's true. You should be in movies. You'd put all those others to shame.

TERRI
Ohhhhh, I'm going to be very nice to you Mr. Frank Leahy.

FRANK
You already have been.

TERRI
I'm going to do even better.

FRANK
Then stop talking and let's see what can be better....

They roll over into each other's arms, then...(<u>TO THE DISCRETION OF THE DIRECTOR</u>.)

FADE TO:

To the Discretion of the Director part V

This is by far my favorite "to the discretion of the director" note in the screenplay, as Wood leaves it up to the director to decide just how much of a sex scene is going to be in this picture. It's highly reminiscent of Ric Lutze's memories of lines like "go into sex" in the *Necromania* screenplay.

It's hard to tell if Wood just couldn't help himself or if he was under instructions to include a little sex. If he was under instructions, it seems like a strange instruction for a football screenplay, though the source material, as mentioned before, does include a couple lines hinting at Leahy's prowess between the sheets and success with women.

FL - 72

148. EXT. RALLEY - (NOTRE DAME vs ?) - WIDE - ESTABLISHING - NIGHT

The bon fire rages and the students are wild in their glee. There are both male and females since it is a co-ed school.

149. MEDIUM TWO - FRANK & MOON MULLINS

Watching the activity as a young man comes up behind them and taps MOON MULLINS on the shoulder. This is young JOHN CAVANAUGH (who will become a Priest and very important to the story from this point on.)

CAVANAUGH
What's a good Catholic like you doing in enemy territory.

MULLINS spins on him and his face lights up. They greet each other with heavy hand shakes and pats on the back...all very broad.

MULLINS
John Cavanaugh...well what do you know about that!!!

CAVANAUGH
You are evading my question.

MULLINS quickly looks to a couple of co-eds as they dance by them.

MULLINS
Well now John. We heard there was some pretty good stuff around here and we thought we'd come and see for ourselves.
(suddenly indicates Frank)
John, this is my best pal Frank Leahy. Frank, John Cavanaugh...

They shake hands.

John is a seminary student.

FRANK
Is that a fact! I've always had great admirations for those in your line.

CONTINUED

Enter John Cavanaugh

In this scene we meet perhaps the third most important character in the screenplay after Leahy and Rockne, John Cavanaugh. Wood notes here that he later becomes a priest and very important to the story. In fact, Cavanaugh became prefect of religion at Notre Dame in 1931, became vice president of the university in 1940, and was finally president of the school in 1941. He resigned in 1952 but stayed associated with Notre Dame as the director of the Notre Dame Foundation. He also served as informal chaplain to the Kennedy family – yes, *that* Kennedy family.

In this screenplay, he's the most memorable character after Rockne, well drawn and warmly written, portrayed as Leahy's closest ally, advisor and best friend.

In Williams' book, Leahy relates meeting Cavanaugh at a lunch in Washington, D.C. He says it was the most important meeting of his entire life, and that instantly he and Cavanaugh had a connection and had so much to discuss Leahy was almost late for the bus to a game against the Navy.

Here, Wood has the two meet at a pep rally bonfire through mutual friend "Moon" Mullins. Credit goes to Wood for devising a more cinematic setting for the meeting.

Although this film never went into production, a movie featuring John Cavanaugh as a character did eventually make it onto the big screen in the form of 1993's *Rudy* with actor Robert Prosky as Cavanaugh.

FL - 73

149. CONTINUED

JOHN
I've always had the same admiration. I guess that's why I want to be one.

FRANK and JOHN laugh. MULLINS takes a flask from his pocket and hands it to FRANK who takes it.

CAVANAUGH
I'd love to have gone to Notre Dame. It represents all to me which is Catholic.

FRANK drinks.

But you're really representing the Catholics out there on the gridiorn.

MULLINS indicates the flask to JOHN.

CAVANAUGH
None for me, thank you, Moon.

FRANK
The religious significence of that game tomorrow was made quite clear by the Coach.

CAVANAUGH
How is Coach Rockne? Is he here tonight?

FRANK
(clouding)
The coach is in the hospital.

Forgetting his friends MULLINS suddenly latches on to one of the girls who is passing/ She accepts him broadly with a kiss and taking his arm. They go off.

He's been having some leg troubles... Clotting and that sort of thing.

CAVANAUGH
(honestly)
I trust it won't turn into anything serious.

CONTINUED

Burying the Lede

As an aside, in the midst of the first meeting of Leahy and Cavanaugh, Wood has Leahy casually drop the bomb that Rockne is in the hospital. It's almost as if Wood is deliberately attempting to avoid showing any important dramatic moments in the lives of these characters, focusing on sequences involving college pranks and Leahy's love life in favor of major things like a towering character like Rockne ending up in the hospital.

FL - 74

149. CONTINUED

FRANK
(as if he'd never thought of such a thing)
God! I hope not!

150. WIDE

The opponent's Varsity players make a big noise as they join the action. They all wear big "D" on their sweaters. Even MULLINS cheers them.

151. MEDIUM TWO - FRANK & CAVANAUGH

Looking off scene toward the re-newed action.

FRANK
Look at that crazy lug...cheering the enemy.

CAVANAUGH
I suppose he's a lot like me. I admire all football players. It's a rough sport, you've got to have courage...
(then he quotes)
"Cowards die many times before their death; the valient never taste of death but once."

FRANK
Shakespeare.

CAVANAUGH
(nods)
Julius Ceasar.
Life has little more of importance then finding goals consistent with God's laws, and then putting all of your energies, your heart, your mind and sour into achieving those goals.

FRANK
When you get to preaching you're sure going to be one inspiration to your congregation.

CONTINUED

Shakespeare

Wood has Cavanaugh quote Shakespeare's *Julius Caesar* (though he spells "Caesar" incorrectly). Interestingly, Leahy references *Julius Caesar* in Williams' book, as well, but it's in a completely different context, comparing the team's reaction to him riding to Notre Dame on a horse with "the mob scene from Shakespeare's *Julius Caesar*."

FL - 75

151. CONTINGUED

CAVANAUGH
(grins)
You know I don't mean your goals might not alter a bit as you learn and mature.

FRANK
Don't worry. I get the point. But I'm determined to beat every obstacle to achieve my goals. I'm going to use my God-given talents to the fullest.

CAVANAUGH pats him on the shoulder.

CAVANAUGH
See you at the game tomorrow.

FRANK
You bet. And I gotta be going too. I don't like to play around too long before a big game... See you...Padre...

They shake hands and go off in their own directions.

152. INT. END OF TUNNEL - LONG SHOT - DAY

The CAMERA is shooting the length of the tunnel looking out to the football field at the far end. Several figures are seen to enter...one is on a stretcher and as we get closer we see a DOCTOR, an ASSISTANT COACH, and a couple of men carrying a stretcher. FRANK, in pain, is on the stretcher.

153. INT. DRESSING ROOM - WIDE - DAY

FRANK is taken from the stretcher and placed on a table. Hê is holding his elbow and is in tremendous pain. The DOCTOR prepares a hypo and the ASST. COACH LOOKS ON.

ASST. COACH
Bad Doc.

DOCTOR
Bad enough...but nothing permanent I'd say. We'll ship him down to the hospital for X-rays and some bandaging anyway.

CONTINUED

Off Screen Injury

Once again, Wood cuts from a line anticipating an upcoming game not to the game itself, but sideline action as Leahy is carried off the field with an injury. Rather than showing the in-game action that caused Leahy's injury, we cut directly to the aftermath. In two almost consecutive scenes we've had both of our main characters either fall ill or get injured off screen, rather than on.

Oddly enough, Wood's description of the shot composition – the camera shooting the length of the tunnel looking out to the football field – is evocative and cinematic and would make a fine shot, so it's baffling that he conceives of this visually, but skips over the injury itself. Again, maybe he was under instructions to avoid in-game action for budgetary reasons, but I suspect he may have just been uncomfortably out of his element.

FL - 76

153. CONTINUED

CAVANAUGH
Don't fight it.

FRANK
Damn...pardon the expression
Padre, but I just gotta play
that game next Saturday. My
folks are coming to see me
play. They've never seen me
play before...

His voice trails off after than and he passes out. The DOCTOR comes in to check his pulse and heart beat, etc., and is satisfied...

FADE TO:

154. INT. HOSPITAL ROOM - MEDIUM CLOSE - PULL BACK TO WIDE - DAY

KNUTE ROCKNE is propped up with pillows on his bed as he reads the sports pages. The door opens and FRANK sticks his head in.

FRANK
Busy?

KNUTE looks to him and his face lights up. He puts the paper over his legs.

KNUTE
Not to you. Come on here you
hot-footed bastard. You're
a sight for sore eyes.

FRANK comes in, closes the door. He carries some Roses.

Nothing around here but them
in the white coats and starched
collars...not a smell of swaat
among the lot of them.

FRANK
(grin)
Yet a football player takes more
baths than all of them put
together.

CONTINUED

FL - 77

154. CONTINUED

They both laugh.

KNUTE
Roses!

FRANK
Roses!

KNUTE
I always liked Roses. That's what I took the Gipper when he was down on his back.

FRANK
I didn't know that.

KNUTE
Something the press neglected to print...they don't neglect much, do they?

FRANK
Not much.

KNUTE
Put them over there on the stand and I'll get one of the nurses to put them in something for me.

FRANK
Good looking ones?

KNUTE
Who?

FRANK
The nurses?

KNUTE
Some around I guess. I get the old bats. They're afraid to let the pretty young ones in here alone with me.

FRANK
There you are all laid up like you are and all you think about is dolls...

CONTINUED

FL - 78

154. CONTINUED

KNUTE
Hey boy...it's only my legs that's in bad shape.

FRANK
How are the legs?

KNUTE
Comin' real nice. Get outta' here in a couple of days. Point comes now. How are you?

FRANK
I heal fast.

KNUTE
How fast?

FRANK
Fast enough for the game with S.C., on Saturday.

KNUTE
Like hell.

FRANK
But Coach...

KNUTE
Don't but Coach me...No game until I'm positive that elbow is healed but good.

FRANK
It was only a sprain. And asprin takes care of everything now. Not even a joint to pull. I tell you it's A-okay.

KUNTE
That ain't what Hunk tells me.

FRANK
Hunk is a worry-wart. I got to play that game. My whole family is coming to see me play for the first time. I can't disappoint them. My Dad always wanted me to be a boxer...was always against me playing foot-

CONTINUED

FL - 79

154. CONTINUED

FRANK (cont'd)
ball. Now's my chance to show him, maybe not that he was wrong, but I was right.

KNUTE
(seriously)
Can't you tell them to come down for some later game.

FRANK
Too late...

KNUTE
Oh...

FRANK
Besides the S.C., game is a big and a tought one...the kind of game I'd like to have them see me in when they're seeing me for the first time.

KNUTE
Yeah...I can see what you mean!!! But a player ain't no good if his wing is clipped.

FRANK flexes his LEFT ARM wildly. This of course is not the arm he had hurt.

FRANK
Can a bad arm do that.

KNUTE
Let me take a look at it.

FRANK crosses to him and KNUTE puts the arm through some strenuous movements...then let's it go.

Hey boy, I put that arm through some rough treatment and I watched you eyes. You didn't even flinch. You might fool me otherwise...but they didn't fool me...not the eyes.

FRANK has a moment of uneasiness.

They didn't even blink.

CONTINUED

FL - 80

154. CONTINUED

FRANK
(brightening)
Then I can play?

KNUTE
(grin)
You know what's best for you!

FRANK
Pa's sure gonna change his
tune now...

WIPE DISSOLVE TO:

155. INT. RUSTIC SPEAK-EASY - WIDE - NIGHT

A man at the door...all men customers...some at tables, some at the bar where no bottles are in sight...all drink from coffee cups. LEAHY SR., is prominent at the bar. He has a drink in front of him but he is not drunk...simply a sociable drinker. The BARTENDER goes to him.

156. CLOSE TWO LEAHY SR., & BARTENDER

BARTENDER
Another beer Frank?

LEAHY SR.
(shakes head)
Moderation in all things I always
say.

BARTENDER
Yeah, that's what you always do
say alright...You sure must be
proud of that son of yours Frank!

LEAHY SR.
The only prouder I could be was
if I had heard him bein'
announced boxing champion of
the world today instead of
being a football hero. But
that's what he wanted...
(winks)
Damn good, wasn't he?

CONTINUED

Sleight of Arm

This sequence reflects a story Leahy relates in Williams' book. Just like in the book, an injured Leahy wants to get back into action prematurely, so he can play in a game his whole family is coming to see. To do so, he allows Rockne to examine his arm. Satisfied, Rockne gives the green light for Leahy to play. The trick is, Leahy offered up the healthy arm for inspection rather than the injured one, in another moment of crying wolf.

In the book, this scene takes place in Rockne's home, where he's bedridden. In the screenplay, this scene takes place in the hospital, which gives Wood a chance to have Leahy and Rockne make some locker room talk about the nurses.

Later in the screenplay, Rockne makes it clear to Leahy that he knew he was lying about his arm, but wanted him to play because he knew how important it was to him. In the book, Leahy speculates this might be the case, but it is never confirmed.

FL - 81

156. CONTINUED

BARTENDER
That S.C., mob is tought to beat.

LEAHY SR.
I was supposed to be there.

BARTENDER
I know. How come you didn't go? I'd close the joint up to go to a game like that.

LEAHY SR.
Oh, I don't know. I thought about it a long time...Only got interested in the danged sport 'cause of young Frank...then agin' I'm past eighty...travel don't agree with me much anymore. Some of the others went. But Ma stayed back with me...Just as soon listen to it on that there radio of yours.

BARTENDER
Ain't you got no radio out at your place Frank?

LEAHY SR.
Sure! Ma listens to it all the time, but she won't allow beer in the house. I like a beer now and agin'...specially when I listen to the games.

LEAHY SR., takes a parge pocket watch from his vest, then replaces it.

Looks about time I get on up the road. Ma'll have supper ready.

BARTENDER
When's the next game?

LEAHY SR., pulls a wad of bills from his pocket.

157. CLOSE TWO - HEAVIES

TWO ROUGH LOOKING CHARACTERS are seated, with beers in

CONTINUED

FL - 82

157. CONTINUED

front of them, at a shadowy table near the rear of the establishment. They acknowledge to each other what they have seen.

LEAHY SR. (o.s.)
Donno...I'll find out for you?

158. MEDIUM TWO - ANGLED - LEAHY SR., & BARTENDER.

While LEAHY SR., is PAYING THE BARTENDER, the TWO MEN can be seen getting up from the table. They walk behind LEAHY SR., on their way to the front door, glance at him as he puts his money back into his pocket then continue on out of the scene.

The BARTENDER returns with the change and LEAHY SR., stuffs that into his pocket with the rest of his money.

BARTENDER
Take care Frank!

LEAHY SR.
Be sue-ing ya'!

BARTENDER
(startled)
What?

LEAHY SR.
Beats me...just heard some kids
say it...called slang...something
new the kids say...got to keep
up with the kids these days....

He laughs and starts out.

159. EXT. SPEAKEASY - WIDE - NIGHT

The small farm village is quiet. LEAHY SR., comes out into the crisp night air, looks to the dark sky and breaths deeply, then starts in the direction of his farm, out of town....

160. EXT. DIRT ROAD - MEDIUM - MOVING - NIGHT

The CAMERA MOVES along with LEAHY SR., as he trudges

CONTINUED

FL - 83

160. CONTINUED

along the dirt road...He spies a tin can in front of him, stops, eyes it, then makes a kick run and with the toe of his boot he sends the tin can flying off into the fields...

LEAHY SR.
(scowling)
Football!!!!

The scowl slowly disappears and he breaks into a grin... the grin into a broad smile...the smile into a light laughter and the laughter into the bellowing laughter of pure humor, pride and happiness....

161. EXTREME HEAD CLOSE - LEAHY SR.

The laughter exploding from him with the tears beginning to stream down his cheeks...UNTIL...The club lands squarely at the back of his head....

162. MEDIUM - SCENE

The TWO HEAVIES seen at the bar are not satisfied with the club to the back of the man's head...besides he has not gone down. The one clubs him over and over while the other drives fists into his face and into his guts. LEAHY SR., attempts at battling back, but he is an old man for all his size. He is no match for the blows and he goes down. The TWO HEAVIES kick and grind their feet into him...and when he is still on the ground they strip him of all his cash and his watch, then with one last kick to the already dead man's middle they race back into the woods at the side of the road.

DISSOLVE TO:

163. EXT. GRAVEYARD - WIDE - DAY

The services for LEAHY SR., are just ending. The family are all there, wives, children, etc., along with friends and the PRIEST. The casket, a simple affair, rests over

CONTINUED

The Death of the Father

Wood has set up Leahy's excitement of his family, specifically his father, finally getting to see him play, only to now dash those hopes as Leahy's father opts to listen to the game on a radio at a speakeasy rather than showing up. The image of Leahy's father "prominent at the bar. He has a drink in front of him…" seems straight out of a similar shot in *Glen or Glenda*, in which Glen's unloving father drinks at the bar.

In Williams' book, Leahy relates that his father died at the age of 73, when Leahy was in his late 20s and well out of college. Here, Wood has moved the death to the middle of Leahy's college career and inflated his father's age to over 80. Moving the death to Leahy's college years has clear reasoning behind it, creating a more dramatic sequence of events than real life had to offer. Inflating Leahy's father's age, on the other hand, is inexplicable.

According to Leahy in Williams' book, Leahy's father was beaten to death in a mugging. Wood keeps this general incident, but in his bid to continue to pit father against son, moves the tragic assault to the very day Leahy's father was supposed to see him in action and decided not to show up. This is good storytelling instinct, but Wood fails to cash in on it later as there is no payoff – we never find out how Leahy feels about his father not showing up. There would have been some dramatic irony if we had gotten a scene of Leahy being upset and feeling hatred towards his father for not being there, only to then find out he was beaten to death, and feel guilty for his conflicting thoughts. This might have been Wood's intention, and he might have just forgotten as he sped along, trying to get this job done. Again, this is something that could have been addressed in a second draft.

Unlike scenes involving football, Wood lingers over this speakeasy scene and the subsequent assault in great detail. He must have felt more at home writing about bars and back alley murders, a recurring location and action in his many short stories and novels.

FL - 84

163. CONTINUED

the open grave. MRS. LEAHY has no tears in her sorrow. FRANK stands on one side of her and GENE on the other.

The PRIEST closes his prayer book then goes to shake both GENE and FRANK'S hands and mutters words of condolences, then silently takes both of MRS. LEAHY's hands in his before he goes on to the others of the immediate family.

164. CLOSE THREE - MRS. LAEHY, FRANK & GENE

All are still looking to the off scene casket.

GENE
(lightly)
If it's any consolation, the Sheriff told me just before the services that they caught the two men who killed Pa. They had his watch.

MRS. LAEHY looks to him, then back off scene.

MRS. LAEHY
Mr. Laehy was a very good man... a very good man to all of us.

FRANK
Ma! How come you never called him anything but _Mr._ Laehy?

MRS. LAEHY
(seriously
looks to him)
I suppose for the same reason you boys always called him Dad or Pa! It was the custom when we were first going together...We are all creatures of habit.

She turns them around, takes their arms and....

165. WIDE & HIGH

...walk out of the ancient, but small, graveyard...the others can be seen some distance in advance of them.

FADE TO:

The Funeral

It wouldn't be an Ed Wood screenplay without a graveyard, by far one of his favorite locations. The shadows of grief must have clouded Wood's very reason, here, as he suddenly starts misspelling Leahy as "Laehy" for a couple pages.

FL - 85

166. EXT. PRACTICE FIELD - WIDE - ESTABLISHING - DAY

The men going through their paces with KNUTE ROCKNE on the side lines shouting his orders. The PLAYERS execute them (TO THE DISCRETION OF THE DIRECTOR.) Then....

167. MEDIUM - FRANK & PLAYERS

...FRANK is hit a stunning blow...he goes down...it is his knee...He writhes on the ground in tremendous pain...KNUTE ROCKNE runs into the scene along with the DOCTOR who bends down over it. The DOCTOR looks up to ROCKNE and shakes his head seriously.

WIPE DISSOLVE TO:

168. INT. LOCKER ROOM - MEDIUM - DAY

FRANK'S leg is being bandaged. With the leg being tightly bandaged the terrifying pain has gone although FRANK is far from comfortable.

FRANK
How bad is it Doc?

DOCTOR
Bad enough!

FRANK
Doc, you never cease to amaze me. Haven't you got any other sentences in your vocabulary other than "Bad enough"?

DOCTOR
It seems to serfice.

FRANK
I guess this about does it...

DOCTOR
Does what?

FRANK
Here it is my senior year and if I can't play ball how am I going to attract enough attention to land any kind of worthwhile coaching job?

CONTINUED

On Screen Injury

Although Wood leaves the details of this football practice up to the director's discretion, he does choose to actually dramatize Leahy's injury this time, instead of skipping over it like last time. So, that's an improvement, but two injury scenes in quick succession seems redundant. Why not reduce this down to just one injury for efficiency and dramatic purposes?

For a moment the doctor's "Bad enough!" response struck me as Wood being repetitive, but it turned out the joke was on me – it's a deliberate set up for an intentional joke.

168. CONTINUED

DOCTOR
Thinking about coaching, huh!!!

FRANK
I've decided to make football my life. I never did think I was the best football player to ever run down the field... But I think I'd make one hell of a splash as a coach.

DOCTOR
(grin)
You know Frank...I think you would at that...And off the record...so does Rockne...

FRANK
You ever hear him say......

He is cut off in his question by a loud series of curses and a rumble which only could be brought on by KNUTE ROCKNE...He is carried in by several members of the team, one leg held straight out in front of him...He is in pain but that does nothing to the language he issues as they lay him out on the table next to FRANK. The DOCTOR quickly goes to him and examines the leg.

KNUTE
How bad is it?

DOCTOR
Bad enough....

That's all FRANK can take...he breaks off into peels of laughter....The DOCTOR knows what it's all about and continues with his work but all the others look at him as if he has lost his mind.

WIPE DISSOLVE TO:

169. INT. LOCKER ROOM - WIDE - DAY

KNUTE with his leg in a cast and riding a wheel chair

CONTINUED

FL - 87

169. CONTINUED

while FRANK is on crutches. The team is about ready to get on the field for a game.

KNUTE
Well...good, bad or indifferent boys...I gotta lay it on you like it is. This is a very special game for me because it's my last game...

Shock sets in and the PLAYERS let it out - ad libs...

No...no...no...that's the way it is. You all know I went in for a check up with the doctors again last week. My ticker ain't what it used to be. Fact of the matter is the doctors say it's in pretty bad shape.

More ad-libs of surprise and shock.

The phlebitis jammed some clots in there and the valves are gettin' a little sticky so I'm checking into the hospital tomorrow.... So now it's up to you to make your old coach happy one last time. There's nothing I'd appreciate more than to go out on a resounding winning note....

The PLAYERS cheer him..."We'll do it Coach"..."You got it in your pocket Coach," etc.

170. EXT. GAME - STOCK - DAY

(TO THE DISCRETION OF THE DIRECTOR.)

171. CLOSE GROUP - SIDELINES - FRANK - KNUTE FEATURED

A man stands behind KNUTE'S wheelchair and FRANK stands next to KNUTE. Both their faces are tense. The fans are restless in their off scene acceptance and rejections of the game...KNUTE leans far forward in his chair....

CONTINUED

EXT. GAME – STOCK – DAY (To the Discretion of the Director part VI)

Almost one and a half hours of screen time into the movie we finally get to see an actual football game being played. As Wood would have it, it's presented as stock footage, and he leaves it up to the director to figure it out. To be fair, even a major production like Warner Bros. *Knute Rockne All American* used stock footage for wide shots of football games, but they shot medium angles of in-game action specifically for the movie, featuring the movie's actors, and tried to match it up to the stock footage. Better late than never, I guess. We do cut away from whatever play wins the game, though, to focus on Leahy and Rockne on the sidelines. Still, it's an improvement, if perhaps too little, too late.

FL - 88

171. CONTINUED

There is a tense, almost silent pause in the crowd noises THEN...all hell breaks loose. KNUTE hugs himself with pride. He laughs, he cries, FRANK shakes his hand.... Then KNUTE looks up to FRANK.

KNUTE
You know Frank. I think that win is going to do a world of good for my heart....

FADE TO:

172. EXT. PRACTICE FIELD - WIDE - DAY

KNUTE, in the wheelchair watches the players as they jog out onto the field. FRANK hobbles in from the background on his crutches and he stops near KNUTE who looks up at him.

173. CLOSE TWO - FRANK & KNUTE

KNUTE can't help but notice the depressed attitude FRANK holds as he looks off to the playing PLAYERS.

KNUTE
Want out there, don't ya'?

FRANK
You don't have to ask that. Hey I thought you was checking into the hospital today?

KNUTE
Postponed it a few days. Too much to clean up around here. Holidays are only a few days off...
(pulls heavy coat around him)
The weather sure tells me that.
(pace change)
Look!

CONTINUED

FL - 89

173. CONTINUED

KNUTE (cont'd)
Frank! I don't like to be in those places alone with nobody I can shoot my kind of breeze with. That knee of yours don't seem to be getting any better. Why don't you check in for the Christmas Holidays with me... unless you've got other plans?

FRANK
(eyes brightening)
I've got no other plans.

KNUTE
Then it's settled. I'll make all the arrangments....
(pace change)
Now I've got another problem. Want to do me a favor?

FRANK
You don't have to ask that either.

KNUTE
Hunk didn't show up for practice ...won't until after the Holidays. Problems back home. You know a lot about line-play. How about subbing? Coach a little?

FRANK is really pleased.

FRANK
You bet.

KNUTE
Then what are you waiting for, a formal invitation. Get the hell out there.

FRANK starts hobbling off, but is stopped by KNUTE again.

You know Frank. It wouldn't surprise me one damned bit if one day you got my job...

FRANK grins, waves, then runs off scene to the field.

CONTINUED

FL - 90

173. CONTINUED

One of the ASSISTANT COACHES comes up beside KNUTE.

ASSISTANT COACH
That Leahy is a something go-getter!

KNUTE
Watch it sonny!!! Someday you may be looking to him for a job!!!

FADE TO:

174. INT. HOSPITAL ROOM - MEDIUM - DAY

A NURSE carries in their dinners on a wheel cart to FRANK and KNUTE who are in beds in the two bed room. Both are sitting up, KNUTE has been reading and FRANK making diagrams for future plays. They look to the NURSE.

KNUTE
What kind of a place is this... Who the hell ever heard of serving supper at five o'clock in the after noon...

The NURSE pays little or no attention to him as he continues the tirade she has become used to.

The day is just starting. I don't even let my boys off the field until six. Waste of valuable time. Wait until you get as sick as me and you'll find out how valuable time is.

She puts the supper in position for FRANK and she addresses him.

NURSE
You'll have to turn your phonograph down, Mr. Leahy or I'll have to take it away....

CONTINUED

FL - 91

174. CONTINUED

FRANK
(puzzled)
Phonograph? Phonograph? What phonograph? We don't have a phonograph in here!

She feigns startled and looks around, then eyes KNUTE.

NURSE
Oh! Then it must be Mr. Rockne. I've heard those same words so many times in the last few days I was positive it was a phonograph record...

She twirls and in the sound of stiff startched clothes she crosses and leaves the room.

KNUTE
Bitches...they're all bitches... I hate these places. Man can't be free to do what he wants. Man can't be free then he might just as well be dead!

He looks over the meals.

Slop!

FRANK tastes of his and makes a face...

FRANK
Well, it's for sure they don't like to put any taste in their food.

KNUTE
By damned!!!

He reaches over and grabs up the phone. He jiggles the receiver....

Two-two-one-H-one!!!

FRANK
(grins)
Sound's like football signals.

CONTINUED

FL - 92

174. CONTINUED

KNUTE
Well my friend...
(narrow eyes)
I'm taking the ball and running with it...
(into phone)
Hello...Hunk...The Coach here. What time you planning on coming over here...to hell with visiting hours, that's two hours away...you get your ass over here in fifteen minutes and bring half a dozen cheezeburgers and a couple of pints of beer. Come up the back way...You know how it's done, I don't have to tell you...

He slams up the phone immediately after he has given the orders to his Assistant Coach.

FRANK
(grin)
I like the way you get things done Coach.

KNUTE
Sometimes the only way to get things done is the direct approach...we can't always depend on deceptive measures... Remember that when you're coaching.

FRANK
Anybody who is looking for a coach will have forgotten me by this time. It's been a long time since I played.

KNUTE
Season's not over yet...So you're graduating pretty quick! I'll help you all I can, you know that.

FRANK
Sure...sure, coach, I know.

KNUTE
I should have told Huck to make it in ten minutes. Give him a good run...take some of the beef off his hide.

CONTINUED

FL - 93

174. CONTINUED

KNUTE leans heavily back against the pillows and stretches his arms skyward.

KNUTE

Does you good to lay up in a hospital every couple of years or so...relax...nothing to do.

(looks at Frank)

Expensive though. School takes care of yours, huh?

FRANK

Yeah...Injury in the line of duty and all that sort of thing.

(pace change)

You made any plans Coach?

KNUTE

Ah, sure...

(waves hand)

I always got plans. I always plan ahead. I made a name for myself these past years. I guess kids as well as the grown-ups all over the world know about me. And when you get a name that name can be turned into dough. Producers out in Hollywood want me to do the coach in "Good Times". Studebaker's going to name a car after me and the Hearst people have already offered me seventy-five grand to write a football column.

FRANK

So which have you decided on?

KNUTE

All of them...Why not? They're spaced out so that I can tackle all of them and more if they come along...but first...As soon as I'm out of here I'm flying to Hollywood for that movie job. Guess they didn't get enough of my triades that first time...

(laughs)

...Or maybe they just couldn't believe it and want to see for themselves, the big-wigs out there.

FRANK laughs along with him.

CONTINUED

FL - 94

174. CONTINUED

KNUTE reaches into a drawer of his night stand and takes out several letters and telegrams. He looks at them then puts them on the roll table which contains his supper. He pushes the cart across to FRANK.

KNUTE
Something here might interest you.

FRANK
What are they?

He picks up several at one time and begins to look through them. He becomes excited as he does so.

KNUTE
Requests for me to recommend an assistant coach. Take your pick. You'll find one from your old Freshman Assistant Coach Tommy Mills...Remember Tommy Mills?

FRANK
Well, sure!

KNUTE
He's Coach Mills now...over at Georgetown...needs somebody to shape up his line...and when you shape them up, look deep into there eyes. The eyes don't lie. Remember I told you that once... in a hospital room just like this.

Frank flinches...KNUTE grins at his discomfort.

Oh, I knew about the left and the right elbow...the eyes didn't lie. But you wanted that game so bad I let you go in anyway...The rush is on son, don't wait around for the breaks to come...get out there and grab hold with both fists before somebody else does.

The sound of a TRI-MOTOR airplaine is heard...ghostly... distant.

The rush is on, and nobody is standing still, they're all running for the daylight....

CONTINUED

FL - 95

174. CONTINUED

The tri-motors ever increasing under the dialgoue.

KNUTE
It's a great game, football.
When a person today goes to see
a football game, they can see
what's going on. There's pagentry.
There's an open football field.
You can see all the exciting,
the thrilling, the spectacular
moments of the game all spread
right out there in front of
you...Ahhh, football. It's my
mother, my father and all the
future relatives I'll never
know....

The motor is extremely loud and there is an ear shattering crash and explosion...the terrified screams of people... then....

LONG FADE TO:

175. EXT. FUNERAL - STOCK - DAY

(IF POSSIBLE AND TO THE DISCRETION OF THE DIRECTOR) As the thousands mourn the passing of the great KNUTE ROCKNE of Notre Dame...We hear the Notre Dame Victory March played in dirge style over the proceedings... Newspaper's with their blaring black headlines read, "ROCKNE DEAD" - "ROCKNE DIES IN PLANE CRASH" - "FOOTBALL'S KNUTE ROCKNE IS NO MORE" - "THOUSANDS MOURN ROCKNE."

The papers have filtered onto the screen then disappear only to be followed by another, and another, etc., (TO THE DISCRETION OF THE DIRECTOR.)

The CAMERA begins to PULL BACK and we find that we have been looking at a movie screen in the:

176. INT. PROJECTION ROOM - CAMPUS - MEDIUM TWO - FRANK & MULLINS - D/N

FRANK snaps a switch to the left of the projector and the lights in the room come on and he turns off the projector. Neither of the two men look to each other at the outset.

CONTINUED

The Hospital Sequence

In this section of the screenplay, as in the book it was based on, and real life, Leahy and Rockne spend quality time in the hospital with each other, convalescing from their respective wounds. This is where Leahy has a one-on-one chance to absorb Rockne's wisdom, and finally decides coaching is his destiny.

Narratively, this sequence acts as the part of the hero's journey where he begins his transformation, with the help of a mentor. It ends in death and rebirth – in this case, the death of Rockne and rebirth of Leahy as a coach. Joseph Campbell would have been proud.

The Bell Has Rung Upon Rockne's Great Career

Wood makes Rockne's death impressively and appropriately cinematic while also keeping it off screen. Here he has the best of both worlds – he's budget conscious and creative, at the same time. This is another example of proof Wood was envisioning (and hearing) this movie in his mind as he wrote it, and not just dashing it off without a thought. Here, he has the sound effect of an airplane grow increasingly louder as Rockne gives his passionate final speech, until the soundtrack is finally taken over by the sound of the airplane crashing at the speech's end.

Rockne did die in a plane crash in 1931, on his way to Hollywood (as in the screenplay) to consult on *The Spirit of Notre Dame*, not to star in whatever *Good Times* was.

One of the most interesting differences between book and screenplay comes here. The book includes a section in which Leahy reveals Rockne was really on his way to conduct an extra-marital affair when he died. Apparently Williams thought this was enough of a bombshell to try to sell the book on it, as this fact appeared in press notices about the book at the time. It's another example of the strange balance the book has between revering Leahy and Rockne as perfect specimens and also revealing scandalous stuff about them. Of course, Rockne could have easily been flying to Hollywood both to have an affair *and* consult on a movie.

This is interesting because Wood makes no reference to it here at all. This is especially interesting when you take into account a later scene in which Leahy cheats on his wife, and an earlier scene in which Wood goes out of his way to trash the reputation of George Gipp, even though the book he's adapting doesn't.

FL - 96

176. CONTINUED

MULLINS
You've been running that film over and over for more than a week Frank.

FRANK
(sigh)
Yeah...I know...I just can't bring myself to believe he's gone.

MULLINS
He's dead Frank, like in
(spells)
D_E_A_D!!!

FRANK
I know...I know...Yet I can't help but think that he'll find a way out of this, that he'll come walking right through that door over there starting his instructions even before he's standing in front of us...I get that feeling he's going to come right up to me on the street on the campus, wherever, and he's going to put his hand on my shoulder and....

MULLINS
Cut it out Frank. That's not healthy...look, you've got that coaching job. He got it for you. One of the last things...maybe the last thing he ever did for anybody on this earth...now you've got to get over there and you've got to make him proud of you...Right after graduation next week that's what you've got to do...that's all you've got to think about...get out there... coach...and win.....

FADE TO:

FL - 97

177. MONTAGE - SCENES

With a couple of different backgrounds as AS FRANK takes players through their routines...(TO THE DISCRETION OF THE DIRECTOR.)

BERNIE (Narration)
(o.s.)
Frank took that assistant coaching job at Georgetown under Tommy Mills and did well, but only well... There were ten scheduled games, four of which they won, one they tied and five they lost. But then...remember Frank wasn't coaching...

178. INT. ROOM - WIDE - NIGHT

FRANK is among several other attending a lecture...On the podium with the speaker is a blackboard with diagrams, the man continually indicates this. His words are not heard on the sound track.

BERNIE (Nar.) (o.s.)
And he continually attended the Coaching Clinics...and above all he was always looking for a better opportunity toward advancement.

179. MONTAGE - SCENES

PLAYERS in routines again, with coach "Sleepy" Jim Crawley in command and Frank and a fellow named CARBERRY. (TO THE DISCRETION OF THE DIRECTOR.)

BERNIE (NAR.) (o.s.)
He next signed as assistant to Sleepy Jim Crawley at Michigan State and when Fordham captured Sleepy Jim he took Frank and a fellow named Carberry with him....

The montage continues with the Michigan State background. But at the point where this NARRATION fit is with a line of seven men coming at us like a block of granite,

CONTINUED

Another Funeral

The "to the discretion of the Director" notes are flying fast and furious by now as Wood takes us through a stock footage and newspaper headline-filled montage of Rockne's funeral, ending with Leahy in a darkened projection room watching and re-watching newsreel footage of Rockne's funeral.

What at first seems like a cheaply cobbled together, cliché-ridden way to represent someone's death, quickly reveals itself to be an homage to *Citizen Kane*. One of Wood's personal heroes was Orson Welles, so he would have likely been familiar with the groundbreaking opening of *Citizen Kane*, which used several different mediums to cobble together the entire story of Kane's life before the picture even really gets going, culminating in his death and a group of reporters watching the newsreel footage in a darkened projection room.

I have to imagine this was an intended homage, but even if it is a subconscious one, we still see Wood bring movies into the picture at a crucial, emotional moment, as if turning to one of his loves is the best way he knows how to interpret Leahy's life. There's nothing in the book about Leahy obsessively watching and re-watching newsreels of Rockne's death – it's all Wood.

In a fascinating coincidence, this is similar to the aftermath of Bela Lugosi's (Martin Landau) death in Tim Burton's 1994 film, *Ed Wood*. In that film, Wood (Johnny Depp) has a little footage left of Lugosi after he dies, and watches it unspool again and again in a darkened projection room, lost in sadness and memory. The cinematography in that sequence (and the rest of the movie) does owe something to *Citizen Kane*, though there is no way Burton or the film's writers, Scott Alexander and Larry Karaszewski, would have known Wood wrote a similar sequence in a screenplay once, and of course no way Wood would know that a scene similar to one he wrote would hit the screen perfectly realized one day.

PL - 98

179. CONTINUED

exact execution of this maneuver (TO THE DISCRETION OF THE TECHNICAL DIRECTOR)

BERNIE (Nar.) (o.s.)
From 1933 to 1938 Fordham won 35 games, lost 8 and tied 7. And it was during the 1936-1937 period Frank designed a line that was so teriffic it was called the Seven Blocks of Granite and became just about as famous as the Four Horesemen of Notre Dame... Even though Frank perfected this play it was credited to Jim Crowley who was the head coach. But it got around the sports world pretty thoroughly that it was Frank's play...

WIPE DISSOLVE TO:

180. INT. FRANK'S ROOM - MEDIUM - NIGHT

FRANK is working over diagrams on his desk under a single night light. From the crumpled up papers around him it is apparent he has been at his task for some time... The page in front of him he also crumples and tosses to the floor and he starts all over again when there is a knock at his door.

FRANK
Who is is?

TOM (o.s.)
Tom Dwyer.

FRANK
(beaming)
Well what the hell....

181. ANGLED

He gets up from the desk and moves to open the door. TOM DWYER, a husky young man, quite good looking comes

CONTINUED

To the Discretion of the Director part VII

These director's discretion notes continue to pick up steam and appear more and more frequently as the narrative moves Leahy out of college and into his coaching career. This also heralds the second return of Bernie Williams as the narrator, his voiceover reappearance coming 64 pages (roughly an hour) since his last voiceover appearance.

If Wood was still following the traditional three act screenplay structure, as he seemed to be at the end of act one, we'd be nearing the end of act two and ready to go into the final act and resolution of the film, with the narrator's reappearance signaling us to that fact. Unfortunately by this point Wood has taken so many pages up with Leahy's childhood and college career that we're not even really halfway through the story of his life.

So, not only is the screenplay running long, but also, Wood seems to be running out of steam. Yes, his creativity pops up here and there, but discretionary notes to the director and now Bernie's voiceovers are taking center stage as Wood rushes us through several years of Leahy's coaching career. It seems like Wood is getting either bored or distracted, or possibly both, and alcohol is probably not helping. It would be interesting to know which pages represent the beginnings/ends of each of Wood's writing sessions. If we knew, we might see the beginning of each writing session correlates with creative, detailed writing and the end of each session ends with confused hackwork.

FL - 99

181. CONTINUED

in and they greet each other broadly before closing the door.

TOM
Hope I'm disturbing you.

FRANK
(joy)
You are.

TOM
So dig out that bottle you've got hidden and buy your old buddy a drink.

FRANK
You got it.

When the door is closed FRANK goes to the rear of the one room establishment and to a make-shift kitchen which has a double hot plate and a small refrigerator. He takes out a tray of ice cubes and takes a bottle from the shelf along with a couple of glasses. The men make themselves comfortable on a couch in the half dark of the room. FRANK pours quickly over the ice then puts the tray of ice and the bottle on the coffee table in front of them.

FRANK
So what's with it boy...what have you been doin1?"

TOM
Not as much as you...Hey, I read the papers. Salute...

FRANK
(tips glass)
Right back at you.

They drink.

TOM
Want a job...something a little extra?

FRANK
The only hard work I do is on the football field these days.

CONTINUED

FL - 100

181. CONTINUED

TOM
Awahhhh. Nothing hard like that!

FRANK
What do you have in mind?

TOM
There's an opening for a sales representative over at the U.S. Rubber Company...

FRANK
I don't know much about selling.

TOM
I've heard some of those lectures you've been giving around. You're a born salesman...big time selling, not like door to door...meet all the big shots...sell big for big commissions.

FRANK
I didn't know anybody knew about my lectures. They aren't publicized but in some hidden back page of local papers.

TOM
I said I heard you lecture. Look it can't do you any harm to look in on it. Say the word and I'll make the appointment for you when I get into my office tomorrow.

FRANK
(thinks but a moment)
Okay...You got the word!

TOM
Then it's settled.

He holds out his empty glass.

Another drink and more news...

FRANK grins and pours both their glasses full again.

CONTINUED

181. CONTINUED

FRANK
Well, there's my part of the arrangment.

TOM
You're working too hard. You need some relaxation.

FRANK
Now that's all according to what kind of relaxation you have in mind.

He forms the human figure with his hands.

TOM
Ala feminine...female...dolls... girls...la petite...

FRANK
Looker's, huh!

TOM
A couple of the best.

FRANK
(winks)
You know I don't go out with just any broad.

TOM
'Course not! 'Course not! Now pal, would I steer you onto a slob.

FRANK
Not my pal Tom Dwyer..no sireee... Only if it would do him some good in the business world. I don't go for blind dates.

TOM
I do admit the match could do me a bit of good...the father of your date owns a big furniture company....

FRANK
(interrupts)
I thought so...count me out.

CONTINUED

Man Alone in a Room

This description of Leahy working under a single light "for some time" with crumpled papers surrounding him sounds very similar to descriptions by Wood's friends and associates of how he would work in Rudolph Grey's *Nightmare of Ecstasy*. Generally, Wood would be drinking and surrounded by people coming in and out while he typed away, but he put in long hours hunched over a typewriter in a shabby room in the solitary act of endless writing. This description recurs multiple times in the upcoming pages, but I wonder if in this moment Wood was basically writing about himself – due to the general sloppiness of the last few pages of the screenplay when Wood finally arrives at this scene, it seems like he was worn out. Maybe he was writing about his own exhaustion here, describing Leahy in the exact position Wood was in, at the time.

As the scene unfolds and Wood goes on to describe the rest of Leahy's place, you can easily imagine him pulling the description right out of his own memories of a string of sad apartments – one room, makeshift kitchen with a hot plate.

Tom Dwyer

Like "Clayton" before him in the early pages of the screenplay, Tom Dwyer comes out of nowhere as an "old friend" of Leahy's we have heretofore never met. He appears twice in Williams' book, instrumental in Leahy meeting his future wife, but here he offers Leahy a job with the U.S. Rubber Company, before moving on to the important business of introducing him to his future wife. In Williams' book, it's a Tom *Young* who hooks Leahy up with his rubber job, so either Wood has his Toms confused or, after a few pages of dutifully summarizing several years of Leahy's life, has chosen to create a composite character.

FL - 101

181. CONTINUED

TOM gulps the drink then takes up the bottle from the coffee table and pours another.

TOM

No, no, now wait. I've seen this chick. I mean she's a doll a real living doll...Irish and Catholic, just like you...names Florence Reilly. Ann...you remember Ann McCafferty...we made up again...anyway Ann introduced me to her couple of weeks back and right away I thought of you. We're invited to her place for dinner this Saturday. Her folks are out of town for the weekend so we'll have the whole place to ourselves.

FRANK

You're luring me into a trap.

TOM

Ahhhh, but a velvet trap. Look! What do you have to lose?

FRANK

Maybe my ass....

DISSOLVE TO:

182. INT. FLOSS' HOME - WIDE - NIGHT

A luxurious home. The door chimes are ringing and the lovely FLORENCE REILLY, a reddish-blonde, dressed beautifully crosses to open it for FRANK, TOM AND ANN. She greets TOM first, kisses ANN on the cheek then as TOM closes the door behind them she turns to look fully at FRANK. TOM steps in quickly.

TOM

Flo, this is my old classmate from Notre Dame, the big Irish mick I've been wanting you to meet. Frank Leahy, Florence Reilly.

CONTINUED

FL - 102

182. CONTINUED

FLOSS

Hi!

She extends her dainty hand and FRANK takes it briefly, holding it as if it might break in his big paw.

Come on in to the living room... all of you.

She leads the way into the spacious, well furnished living room where they will seat themselves in positions which is close enough for easy conversation. TOM speaks on the move and the CAMERA PANS or TRUCKS with them.

TOM

Frank's a big man these days... The sole inventor and creator of the famous Seven Blocks of Granite!

FLOSS

Oh, then you sculpt!

FRANK

(laughs - suddenly feels more at ease)

Nothing so romantic. I'm just an assistant coach...football...over at Fordham.

TOM

Ahh, don't you listen to him Flo. He's just being modest. He's always like that when somebody tells about his accomplishments. I tell you those Seven Blocks of Granite can't be beat. They're the meanest, toughest, defensive line ever put together...and Frank there, sitting right beside you is the man that put it all together.

FRANK

(embarrassed and slightly irritated)

Ah, come on now Tom...cut it out!

CONTINUED

FL - 103

182. CONTINUED

ANN catches the irritation in the air.

ANN
You do that Tom. Flo doesn't know anything about football.

TOM
Okay...on to other stuff! Now where I come from when guests are invited to a house for dinner there are always before dinner drinks as well as after.

FLOSS
(quickly standing)
Ohhh, forgive my manners. I seldom touch it but Dad qeeps quite a supply...but he only drinks burbon.

TOM
That will do just great.

TOM from the very beginning always seems on a high plain, always on stage, full of energy, ready for anything.

FRANK
(nods)
Fine.

ANN
Just a small one.

She crosses the room to a cabinet which opens up into a small bar.

WIPE DISSOLVE TO:

183. INT. SAME - LATER - MEDIUM - NIGHT

The four are at the door preparing to leave. FLOSS says her "so-longs" to ANN and TOM and they start out.

FRANK
I'll be along in a minute.

TOM
(sly wink)
Did your old pal treat you right or did he treat you right!

CONTINUED

FL - 104

183. CONTINUED

FRANK
(grin)
He treat me right old buddy, he treat me right.

FLOSS has heard all this and she also grins, knowing the implications of the words.

TOM
See you in the car...
(knudges him in the ribs)
Take your time...

TOM goes out after ANN who has already gone. FLOSS Comes in close to FRANK.

FRANK
Well...Well it sure was a fine evening...and dinner...thanks for the drinks...

FLOSS
You know Mr. Leahy...

FRANK
Frank...

FLOSS
Frank...pardon me for being forward...I'm really not this way at all, but something about you... you're the best looking football coach I've ever met.

FRANK
Did you ever meet one before Floss..?

FLOSS
(startled)
Floss?

FRANK
I like it better than Flo. Well did you ever meet a football coach before?

CONTINUED

FL - 105

183. CONTINUED

FLOSS
(shakes her head
"No")
But even if I had I doubt very much if he would be nearly as attractive as you.

FRANK
(grin)
They tell me that some of the best looking men around are football coaches.

FLOSS
<u>They</u>? Who are <u>they</u>?

FRANK
The football coaches.
(quickly)
You like movies?

FLOSS
I love movies.

FRANK
Tomorrow night?

FLOSS
(shakes head)
Busy!

FRANK
First I'm attractive, then I get the brush-off.

She quickly takes his hand, seriously thinking she is going to lose him.

FLOSS
Oh, no, nothing like that. It's my sister's birthday...the family and all that sort of thing. How about Friday?

FRANK grins....

DISSOLVE TO:

FL - 106

184. MONTAGE OF SCENES

FRANK and FLOSS at the movies...drinking sodas at a drug store...walking...riding in a car...amusement park... etc., (<u>TO THE DISCRETION OF THE DIRECTOR</u>.) INTER-CUT with FRANK and the players on the football practice field at FORDHAM.

WIPE DISSOLVE TO:

185. INT. MOVIE THEATRE - MEDIUM - D/N

The flickering light from the screen is the only illumination on the young couple. However behind them is a YOUNG STUDIOUS TYPE fellow. The voices from the screen come over the entire scene as well as the music...(<u>FILM TO THE DISCRETION OF THE DIRECTOR</u>.) Both FRANK and FLOSS have large bags of popcorn in their hands. FRANK frees the other hand from hers and he reaches into his pocket. He produces a small box and upon opening it we see that it contains not only ~~a wedding ring~~ an engagement ring, but a wedding ring.

FRANK
(low)
Floss...

FLOSS
Shhhhhh. This is one picture I'd like to see.

FRANK
But it's important.

FLOSS
It can wait.

FRANK
But it can't....

He quickly takes her left hand and puts the engagement ring on the third finger.

YOUNG MAN
(whispering)
Please be quiet....

FLOSS
What's that?

She holds up the diamond engagement ring on her finger so that it sparkles in the projection light.

CONTINUED

Enter Florence "Floss" Reilly

Now we've come to the first meeting of Leahy and his future wife, Florence "Floss" Reilly, who he would stay with until his death. She passed away four years after him, and they're buried together in Portland, OR.

The basic framework of their meeting matches the story laid out by Leahy in Williams' book, though Dwyer's crude introduction of Leahy in the screenplay stands in stark contrast to his introduction in the book.

Screenplay: "Flo, this is my old classmate from Notre Dame, the big Irish mick I've been wanting you to meet."

Book: "Well, here he is, Flo, the fighting Irishman of the century. I've been trying to get him here for a long time to meet you."

Floss was five years Leahy's junior. Although the screenplay is written as if Dwyer and Leahy are infiltrating Mom and Dad's house while they're away and Floss is unguarded, Floss and Leahy would have both been in their 20s when they met and married, so it was not a cradle-robbing situation.

In the screenplay, Wood has Leahy create the nickname "Floss," saying he prefers it to "Flo." In the book, Floss does go by Flo at their first meeting, but it's never made clear where the "Floss" nickname comes from.

In the book, Williams notes that when he knew Floss in the 70s, she reminded him of the actress Thelma Ritter. Ritter is probably most famous as James Stewart's nurse in *Rear Window*. Unfortunately, by the time *The Frank Leahy Legend* would have gone into production, she had already passed on.

FL - 107

185. CONTINUED

She suddenly gets it...and throws her arms around him and kisses him heatedly.

YOUNG MAN
Can't you two be quiet....

They pay no attention to him.

FLOSS
You haven't even asked me yet!

FRANK
Doesn't look like I have to...

FLOSS
Guess you don't at that...When?

YOUNG MAN
I'll report this to the manager.

FRANK
(ignoring the young man)
Tomorrow.

FLOSS
(shock)
Tomorrow? But we've only just gotten engaged.

YOUNG MAN
Ohhhhhhhhhh.
(frustration)

FRANK
You've got all night to be engaged.

FLOSS
But my mother...my father?

FRANK
They'll still be around...later... you can tell them then...

She squeals with delight again and once more throws her arms around his neck and they kiss wildly.

CONTINUED

FL - 108

185. CONTINUED

YOUNG MAN
The balcony is for things like that....
(disgusted)

They part but remain very close.

FRANK
It won't be easy. At least in the beginning. An assistant coach doesn't make much money and I'll be spending three quarters of my life on a football field.

FLOSS
It's the other quarter I'm interested in...

She kisses him again.....

YOUNG MAN
Goddddddddd!

They break their clinch and look at the YOUNG MAN. BOth stand up, retrieve their bags of popcorn. They turn on him and both dump the popcorn all over the hapless young man, then gaily leave the theatre, holding and swinging their hands and arms....

DISSOLVE TO:

186. INT. JUSTICE OF THE PEACE OFFICE - CLOSE GROUP - DAY

FRANK, FLOSS, JUSTICE, WITNESSES. The plain ceremony is coming to a conclusion.

JUSTICE
...thus on this Fourth day of July in the year of our Lord, Nineteen Hundred and Thirty-Six, I hereby pronounce you Frank William Leahy, Junior and you Florence Ann Reilly, man and wife....

They lock into each other's arms for the wedding kiss.

FADE TO:

The Proposal

In both the book and screenplay, Leahy and Floss' first date after their initial meeting is a movie, but Wood goes a step further and takes us to the movies with the couple, even going so far as setting Leahy's proposal there. This is another instance where the world of the movies is injected into Leahy's life by Wood at an important moment.

Like the scene with Henny before this, the main action in the movie theater (the proposal) is offset by a young man sitting behind our main characters. In the Henny sequence, a young man sitting behind Leahy makes off with Leahy's date. In this sequence, Leahy and his date get the best of the young man, dumping their popcorn on him. It's genuinely funny when the young man's annoyed at the proposal, but the punch line of the popcorn dump falls a little flat.

Note Wood's descriptive powers really come to life when setting the scene of the movie theater: "The flickering light from the screen is the only illumination on the young couple." Even the engagement ring itself "sparkles in the projection light."

The Wedding

In the screenplay, Wood has Leahy and Floss married at the "justice of the peace office" in a plain ceremony, on July 4th, 1936.

In the book, while Leahy says they eloped and had a quiet ceremony, it is performed by Reverend Joseph Scanlan, S.J. at St. Patrick's Church in the Bronx on July 4th, 1935, one year earlier.

FL - 109

187. INT. BASKETBALL COURT - WIDE - DAY

Several BUSINESSMEN TYPES are gathered on the court and have been listening to FRANK'S speech which is coming to a finish...

FRANK
Therefore seeing is believing gentlemen, all you coaches and backer's alike. I want to show you just what the rubber sole the U.S. Rubber Company has come up with can do for your basketball players....

Two men come onto the court in basketball uniforms. One is wearing the pre-runner to the rubber soled shoe and the other, the rubber soled shoe. They go through a routine (<u>TO THE DISCRETION OF THE DIRECTOR</u>) and it is apparent the man with the rubber shled shoe does better footwork....Then the PLAYERS leave the floor. One of the men approaches FRANK.

188. CLOSE TWO - JOE & FRANK

JOE
Guess that proves your point, huh, Coach.

FRANK
(grin)
Just put in your order Joe.

JOE
That goes without being said. How's the family?

FRANK
Frank the III is sprouting like a weed...Susan's still in the crib and Floss is by far the best cook in the world.

JOE
The utterances of a happy man. Fordham?

FRANK
Keep your money there...I've got the best line yet....

DISSOLVE TO:

FL - 110

188. INT. LEAHY LIVING ROOM - MEDIUM - NIGHT

A modest apartment living room. FRANK is working at the living room table under a single lamp as he usually does. FLOSS comes through a door near the rear of the room. She closes it carefully, almost silently, then goes up to put her arms around FRANK'S neck. He looks up to her, away from his diagrams.

FRANK
Kid's alright?

FLOSS
Sleeping...like babies...

He gives a light laugh.

Why don't you come to bed.?.you've worked at those <u>things</u> long enough.

FRANK
Those <u>things</u> as you call them are the bread and butter for this house.

FLOSS
(sigh)
I'd like to try for cake and whipped cream for a change.

FRANK
In time, Floss.

FLOSS
I know honey. I'm not complaining. You do try so hard. And you are away so much of the time...Come on to bed...

FRANK turns and lightly thumps her on the rump.

FRANK
Hell girl...it's hard enough for me to feed the mouths I have around here already.

She playfully slaps him on the shoulder as she pulls away...

FLOSS
Oh, you....

CONTINUED

FL - 111

188. CONTINUED

It is at this time that the phone rings. FLOSS goes to the phone stand and picks it up.

FLOSS
(into phone)
Hello...Oh, just a moment.

She cups her hand over the mouth piece and turns to FRANK.

A Mr. Curley want's to talk to you...are you in?

FRANK barely has time to take a double-take as he bolts out of the chair and takes the phone from her hand.

FRANK
(into phone)
Jack...Well you old football thief, What'da ya' say and what'da ya do?
(long pause)

FLOSS knows by FRANK'S attitude that the call is important, but she is puzzled. FRANK'S face brightens all the time he is talking.

You got a deal Jack...Sure you can count on me. I give you my word. Sure it will be hard to get out of, but I've got an angle. I've been working on it ever since I heard you called Southerland and he told you his Pittsburg team was tired of going up against Fordham and Leahy. Yeah, I got my own set of boys...See you Monday!

He hangs up and FLOSS comes in quickly....

FLOSS
What is it.?.what's all the excitement? I haven't seen you this excited in years?

He waves her to be silent as he dials the long distance operator.

CONTINUED

Phone Calls: The Motion Picture

"It is at this time that the phone rings."

So begins the section of the screenplay I like to call "Phone Calls: The Motion Picture". This is the first of many scenes in which Leahy's at his desk working, the phone rings, and a new part of his life begins – a new job, moving to a new city, whatever. A screenplay that started out with honest attempts by Wood to dramatize actual scenes has now devolved into Wood checking off a chronology of events through repetitious, un-cinematic, non-dramatic phone call scenes.

The next call comes on page 116 (and warrants a mention from the narrator), followed by another one on 119. That's three almost identical scenes almost in a row, within less than ten minutes of screen time, moving the action forward in the least imaginative way possible, more hints that Wood is running out of steam on the back half of this screenplay.

FL - 112

188. CONTINUED

FRANK
(into phone)
Give me seven, seven, four, nine, four in ____________ Texas...This is four, zero, six, one, six.
(pause)
DRUZA ~~Bruce~~ boy, this is Frank. Still want to go with me?...Yeah, I got it...contracts on Monday....
(pause)
Well, I figure Mc ~~Ardle~~, ~~Crimmins~~, ~~Earley~~ and ~~Ziemba~~...how's that for a staff? Okay, get to you during the week.

He hangs up and then turns to FLOSS who is nervous in impatient anticipation.

FRANK
(as if she knows what it's all about)
And I won't even loose my job with the U.S. Rubber Company, they have a branch in Boston.

FLOSS
(beyond herself)
Job.?.Boston.?. Frank, what are you talking about?

FRANK
Oh, didn't I tell you. I'm signing on Monday with Boston University as head coach.

She squeels and dives into his arms.

DISSOLVE TO:

189. EXT. FORDHAM PRACTICE FIELD - GROUP - DAY

The PLAYERS are grouped around FRANK for his farewells.

CONTINUED

Handwritten Corrections

Throughout the screenplay so far there have been a few instances of handwritten notes or lines that have been blacked out, but the first line of dialogue on this page represents some of the most scribbling in any one place. My guess is that these particular notes are not Wood's but probably Williams' himself. It looks as if it's possible Wood used the wrong names here and Williams corrected him to make the screenplay more factually accurate.

Specifically, Wood has Bruzo, a name I can't read, Crimmins, Earley and Ziemba mentioned here, and the handwritten notes change it to Druze, McArdle and McKeever, Leahy's assistants at Boston College as mentioned in the book. Crimmins and Ziemba played for Leahy at Notre Dame in the 1940s, so the mention of their names here was anachronistic.

FL - 113

189. CONTINUED

FRANK
And that's it men. Goodbyes are or seem so final so I'll just say so long...and that's the way it should be. Without a doubt we'll be meeting out there on the football field again...only this time...face to face...as <u>enemies</u>...

He laughs and they join in. FATHER JOHN CAVANAUGH in the full rocks of the PRIEST comes up silently behind FRANK.

Okay, so get out there and make this last day of mine a great practice for your school and your head coach Jim Crawley.

The men cheer themselves and run back out of the scene.

CAVANAUGH
Coach Frank Leahy, I presume.

FRANK spins on him....

FRANK
Well I'll be damned, John Cavanaugh!!!
(catches himself)
(eyes him up and down)
Father John Cavanaugh....

The greetings are gay, and warm.

DISSOLVE TO:

190. INT. LEAHY DINING ROOM - MEDIUM - NIGHT

The dinner is over and they are having coffee. FLOSS is not in the room at the moment.

CAVANAUGH
So when I heard about the new Coaching job and here I was in New York, I had to look you up.

CONTINUED

FL - 114

190. CONTINUED

FRANK
And I'm glad you did. I know
Floss was happy to meet you
finally. Guess I talk a lot
about you even though we haven't
seen each other since the bon
fire...I read about you in
the Notre Dame papers.

CAVANAUGH
Yes, I finally did make my way
to Notre Dame even though it
wasn't through football.

FRANK
You stick to your game and I'll
stick to mine...

They laugh and FLOSS comes into the room.

FLOSS
More coffe Father?

CAVANAUGH
Goodness, no...you have been a
most gracious hostess.
(to Frank)
And now you're off to Boston
University...

FRANK
(nods)
End of the week.

FLOSS indicates the packing boxes spaced around the
apartment.

FLOSS
That's why the place is in such
a mess.

CAVANAUGH
(grin)
Moving is always such a chore.
I do hope Notre Dame will be
my permanent home I'd hate to
face moving again.

FRANK
Ahhh, they know a good thing when
they see it. You're in but good.
(pure love)
What a place that Notre Dame.

CONTINUED

FL - 115

190. CONTINUED

CAVANAUGH
Something may be brewing there that you don't know about.

FRANK
Huh?

CAVANAUGH
A lot of people at Notre Dame are keeping an eye on you my boy.

FRANK
Elmer Laydon will never put down the Notre Dame reigns...he'll hold on to them until the day he dies. Hey, what am I going on about. Notre Dame needs all pro...I'm only just starting out on my first job as Head Coach...

CAVANAUGH
A lot of people think you're far ahead of your practical experience, and I wouldn't be too sure about Laydon.
(sigh)
And now I must be going...

FLOSS
Must you Father...It's been wonderful.

CAVANAUGH
Oh yes, I must go. I must admit I'm slightly intimidated by this vast metropolis of strange faces and I long to get back to those more familiar as soon as possible.

FLOSS
Then I feel this is the time to make an announcement. If I don't tell someone...I'll just burst...

FRANK gets the hint but is none the less surprised.

We're pregnant again Frank...

CONTINUED

More Handwritten Corrections

This time, Wood has spelled Elmer Layden incorrectly – someone has corrected his L-e-y-d-o-n to L-a-y-d-e-n. There have been many typos throughout this screenplay, with few of them corrected, so this one stands out. It seems the sin of incorrectly spelling the name of one of the Four Horsemen, and a former Notre Dame football coach, was just too much to ignore.

FL - 116

190. CONTINUED

FRANK
(gulps)
We are?

FLOSS
The doctor confirmed it this afternoon.

CAVANAUGH
Congratulations to the both of you, and I suggest,
(winks at Frank)
...the both of you get more rest.

He starts out....

FADE TO:

191. MONTAGE - FOOTBALL SCENES

Several different games and several different types of plays (TO THE DISCRETION OF THE DIRECTOR.)

BERNIE (NAR. o.s.)
Boston U. held on to Frank for two years, and an impressive two years it was...Then another phone call...

DISSOLVE TO:

192. INT. LEAHY BOSTON LIVING ROOM - MEDIUM - DAY

Much better in styling than the New York apartment, but still not pretencious. The phone is ringing and FLOSS comes out of the kitchen to answer it. She is wearing a night dress and robe.

FLOSS
Hello...Oh, Father John...No, he isn't, but I'll have him call as....

The front door opens and FRANK in evening clothes

CONTINUED

FL - 117

192. CONTINUED

comes in closing the door behind him.

FLOSS
(into phone as she waves Frank over)
Ohh, just a minute Father John, here he comes now.

She holds out the phone to a puzzled frank.

FRANK
Father John?

He takes the phone from her.

(into phone)
John...it's good to hear from you.
(pause)
You're kidding me! No I haven't seen the papers. They gave one of those cocktail parties for me. I just signed a new five year contract...What do you mean get out of it John? I'm going to get out of it. You think I'd miss this one. You just leave that part to me. I've gotten out of contracts before. You just tell Eddie Dunigan your esteemed president I'm all yours baby....

He hangs up and turns to FLO who is obviously pregnant again. He is extremely happy.

Think you're going to like South Bend, Floss?

FLOSS
(happy for him)
Notre Dame?

FRANK
(nods)
Head Coach. Elmer Leydon is quitting to become President of the National Football League... Notre Dame, here I come...

CONTINUED

FL - 118

192. CONTINUED

FLOSS
(clouding)
But...but that new contract with Boston. Curley will never let you out of it...you're too good for that school and he's not going to let you go.

FRANK
He'll have to...Get us a beer.

FLOSS
I don't like beer.

She goes to the kitchen, opens the refrigerator and gets a beer for him. She pops the top and takes it back to him, then picks up a whiskey bottle which is about half full and pours herself an ample shot... she drinks it straight.

FLOSS
Why will he _have_ to let you go?

FRANK
After I make a certain announcement to the papers and over the air he wouldn't dare try to hold me back...not from the juciest spot in the world. He couldn't afford to risk his reputation in not letting me go to Notre Dame.

WIPE DISSOLVE TO:

193. INT. RADIO STATION - ANNOUNCERS BOOTH - CLOSE TWO - DAY

FRANK and the ANNOUNCER are at the mike.

ANNOUNCER
Which brings us to the part of this interview, Frank Leahy, where you said you have something important to tell us.

CONTINUED

Floss Foreshadowing

Wood has Leahy ask Floss for a beer. She mentions she doesn't like beer and pours herself an "ample shot" of straight whiskey. This is the beginning of a subplot featuring Floss' drinking problem. It only has a couple passing mentions in Williams' book. At one point a doctor contacts Leahy to tell him Floss is "hitting the bottle" because Leahy's never home. Williams also notes, "For a while, she had a drinking problem. I will never forget how happy Frank was when he told me that the situation had been completely met."

For as much grief as I give Wood for seeming to go on autopilot, especially in the last half of this screenplay, and allowing characters and incidents to pop up out of nowhere without being properly set up, or setups lacking pay off, it should be noted he attempts to turn these brief mentions of Floss' alcoholism into an ongoing plotline in the screenplay, making sure to pepper references to her drinking throughout so that when the situation comes to a head, it does not come out of nowhere.

So, once again, Wood's both phoning it in and trying to do things right at the same time. The question is, how did he choose what he was going to plot out versus what he was going to just gloss over? It may not have been a conscious choice, and just unfolded haphazardly as he pounded away at the typewriter. Or, it may have been, he took special note of the things that resonated with him. Football, for example, wouldn't have. Alcoholism, on the other hand? He would have been very familiar with that.

FL - 119

193. CONTINUED

FRANK
That I do...That I do. I've just received my release from Boston College, along with their blessings, benedictions, and wishes for nothing but good luck and good fortune at Notre Dame...Thank you....

WIPE DISSOLVE TO:

194. INT. LEAHY LIVING ROOM - CLOSE - DAY - (BOSTON)

The phone is ringing and FRANK moves in to pick it up.

FRANK
Hello Jack...

195. SPLIT SCREEN w/ FRANK'S LIVING ROOM - JACK CURLEY'S OFFICE - DAY

CURLEY
(startled)
How'd you know it was me?

FRANK
I was expecting you.

CURLEY
Okay, you got me over a barrel with that love and kisses stuff. I'm ripping up your contract.

FRANK
Thanks Jack.

CURLEY
Ahhh...
(resgined)
There are other coaches anxious for the job.
(softening)
Good luck, Frank...Make it big.

They both hang up the phones.

FADE TO:

Leahy's Gambit

This sequence is needlessly confusing as written by Wood, but could have been a dramatically satisfying one if handled correctly. Instead it's buried in phone calls. Basically, what Wood's trying to say, is that after signing a new five year contract with Boston College, Leahy gets an offer to coach at Notre Dame, so he gets out of his contract by simply announcing to the press that Boston College already let him out of the contract so he could go to Notre Dame, forcing Boston College's hand.

The story is told a little more adeptly in Williams' book, with Leahy claiming Boston College had said if his Alma Mater ever came calling, he'd be released from his contract, and then going back on it and Leahy trying several legitimate ways to get out of his contract before finally resorting to the tactic featured in the screenplay.

Thematically, Leahy's crying of wolf continues to get him far in the world. This is a strange thing for a sportsman to be proud of – usually, in the realm of athletics, it's all about fair play and may the best man win, cheaters never prosper. Here, cheaters not only prosper but are proud of it. Like James T. Kirk in *Star Trek II: The Wrath of Khan*, Leahy has tricked his way through life and patted himself on the back for his ingenuity. Unlike Kirk, Leahy never comes to the realization that this has resulted in him learning nothing valuable about life.

That's one way of looking at it, of course. Another way of looking at it would be that Leahy was a charismatic character who could talk his way out of and into anything he wanted, which was probably a trait that Wood identified with, to a certain degree, and could have admired. Like Wood, Leahy manifested his successes by not letting anything get in his way and doing whatever it took to get things done. Granted, Wood's successes were minor relative to Leahy's but in his mission to miraculously get his films made against all odds, Wood had to wheel, deal, smooth talk, cheat and lie, just like Leahy.

FL - 120

196. EXT. PRACTICE FIELD - NOTRE DAME - MONTAGE - DAY

FRANK is really putting his PLAYERS through the roughest session of practice we have here-to-fore-seen and the men are not happy about it. They go down and he brings them to their feet...(TO THE DISCRETION OF THE TECHNICAL DIRECTOR.) FRANK'S voice...hard...demanding, comes over the scene.

FRANK (o.s.)
Get up there. What the hell are you a bunch of sissies...You're men and football players at that. I'm not coaching the girls for a prom. You've got a coach now and you're going to learn it but quick. Ziemba, push right through that man. What kind of a dud team did I inherit? It's God's wonder that you ever made a Prep Team...Dig those spikes in. Show me some turf. Get it moving...move...move....

FADE TO:

197. INT. LEAHY'S OFFICE - NOTRE DAME - MEDIUM - DAY

FRANK looks up from his paper work as an almost timid knock comes on the door.

FRANK
Come in.

The man who enters is named LILLIS and he is six foot four and powerful. He wears slacks and shirt with silp-over and letter.

LILLIS
Can I talk to you a minute Coach?

FRANK
I'm kinda' busy, but come on in and speak your piece.

It is almost as if FRANK knows what is about to be said.

CONTINUED

Head Coach, Finally

Finally, about two hours into the film, Leahy has become head coach of Notre Dame, the thing he was most famous for. Under normal circumstances, page 120 of a screenplay would feature the words "The End." In this case, we've still got a ways to go. By contrast, *Knute Rockne All American* clocks in at an efficient 98 minutes.

This is similar to the time Wood was hired to write and direct a sex change movie called *I Changed My Sex*. Instead he gave the world *Glen or Glenda* – a semi-autobiographical tale of cross-dressing, with a little sex change tacked on at the end.

FL - 121

197. CONTINUED

LILLIS
As Captain of the team...

FRANK
(interrupts)
So I know you're Captain of the team Lillis, tell me something new.

LILLIS
You're heading for trouble.

FRANK
Ohhhh.

LILLIS
The men think you're leaning on them to heavily and unless that load is lightened you're going to have a mass resignation of players on your hands.

FRANK
Resignation? How do you mean?

LILLIS
Shoot the whole thing down the sewer pipe...give up their scholarships...quit the team. A lot of the players feel that way.

FRANK stands and becomes hard. He is the coach and they are going to know it.

FRANK
I don't see how you can say what you're saying Paul. You see. I don't have a lot of football players. What I've got is a lot of duds that want to play football...be number one heros without having to work for it. And if we do have a lot of players who want to turn in their scholarships, then they are not the team I've been looking for. You ain't seen nothing yet. Wait until the snow gets on the ground, then

CONTINUED

FL - 122

197. CONTINUED

FRANK (cont'd)
you'll see what work really is. Maybe you think we can't do much with the snow so deep, but you just watch what can be done for football on a basketball court... and that's when the head hunting is going to start before we get down to business with the spring sessions. Now you get back and tell your...PLAYERS... just that.

LILLIS
(flustered)
But...but...coach....

FRANK
And another thing...

He takes up a slip of paper from his desk and hands it across to the man who takes it.

Here's a list of men who are over weight. There are two lists of weights. His present weight and the weight he's going to be. There will be no exceptions. And anyone who hasn't acchieved the designated weight by the end of the Spring practice won't have to resign on his own, he's going to have to resign by my orders, because I'll see that that man never wears a Notre Dame uniform.

LILLIS
(gulps)
My name is on this list.

FRANK
(nods)
Now aren't you ashamed...The Captain of a Notre Dame Football team with the gut of a sow. Now you get out of here and see to your own shape and forget how I'm treating the others. You tell them that...
(pace change)

CONTINUED

FL - 123.

197. CONTINUED

FRANK (cont'd)
On second thought Lillis, why don't you go back to 'em and encourage a lot of them to leave. Encourage them to go home to mama, because the more of 'em that go the stronger the Freshman team will be in the Fall. You just do that little favor for me...Encourage those cry babies to go home.

DISSOLVE TO:

198. EXT. CAMPUS - MEDIUM TWO - TRUCKING - CAVANAUGH & FRANK - DAY

The CAMERA MOVES with FRANK and CAVANAUGH as they walk and talk.

CAVANAUGH
I know you Frank, and I know you want to win, and to win, sometimes you can be...err...rather hard on the boys.

FRANK
I don't force them to play football.

CAVANAUGH
I know but...

FRANK
No buts about it John. They either play the game my way or they don't play for me at all. I played here under the greatest coach who ever lived, Knute Rockne and I am going to come up with even more winning teams then he did. That's the way it is, and that's the way I know he would have wanted it. He made me a coach. He had great faith in me. I won't let him down.

CONTINUED

FL - 124

198. CONTINUED

FRANK (cont'd)
Remember that zero to zero deadlock with Army? I don't appreciate ties...I'd rather lose than tie... but I'm not out to lose.

CAVANAUGH
I'm afraid there is something less than Christian inherent in that attitude.

FRANK
(shrugs)
Winning is the name of my game. And I'm going to introduce an entirely new style next year.

CAVANAUGH
(surprised)
Oh?

FRANK
The Bears have been fooling around with it for awhile, but I think I have it down to a "T"...
(laughs)
Strange thing about it, that's just what it's called. The "T" formation.

CAVANAUGH
Oh, I'd be careful with anything new. You know how the alumni and the powers that be are against anything new. Look you're winning now...You've already been elected Coach of the Year for this 1941 season...why put your head on the chopping block?

FRANK
Because I'm not one for standing still. If I see something new that I <u>really</u> know will work, I'm going to use it...I tell you this "T" is something. It explodes so suddenly from both sides at the same time that it's nearly impossible to stop.

CONTINUED

Less Than Christian

It's nice that Wood allows Cavanaugh to finally point out the moral ambiguity of Leahy's commitment to winning. Leahy literally shrugs it off, but the screenplay at least acknowledges some reasonable people do not think winning is everything.

The T Formation

Wood has Leahy call the T formation "an entirely new style" and gives credit to Leahy for bringing it to college football. While there is passing mention of the Bears already using the formation, which is true to life, the formation is actually one of the oldest offensive formations and goes back to 1882. It did fall out of favor for a while, and bounced back as the Chicago Bears used it from 1920 on and Clark Shaughnessy at the University of Chicago returned it to fame in 1940. Leahy was an advocate for the formation and enthusiastically employed it during his time at Notre Dame, but he didn't invent it and it wasn't new.

Williams' book has Leahy describing how he got wise to the T formation by watching the Chicago Bears play, then personally learned more about it directly from Sid Luckman, then quarterback for the Chicago Bears, who does not appear in this screenplay.

Here, Wood has Cavanaugh warn Leahy about the potential backlash of trying something new, but in Williams' book Leahy has Cavanaugh's blessing.

198. CONTINUED

CAVANAUGH
Well, I know that once your mind is made up, there's no changing it...so God speed and God be with you.

FRANK
Thanks John...see you in a couple of weeks...

CAVANAUGH
(surprised)
Oh, going someplace?

FRANK
Recruiting...There's a couple of boys around who don't know it yet but they're going to play football for Frank Leahy and Notre Dame....

CAVANAUGH shakes his head then laughs....

FADE TO:

199. INT. MEAT MARKET - MEDIUM - DAY

A strapping young fellow with a bloodied apron is cutting up chickens. There are several more, dressed but with the heads still intact on the chopping block next to him. This is SYGMOND "ZIGGY" CZAROBSKI. His father enters the shop from the freezer, a walk in, and he has several more chickens in his hand. ZIGGY is chopping but his mind is elsewhere. The father looks to his son with disgust.

CZAROBSKI
A wedding I got. Twelve chickens fully dressed I need, and there he stands...dreamland he's in yet. Cut boy...cut. The chickens they don't cut off their own heads.

CONTINUED

FL - 126

199. CONTINUED

ZIGGY
I just got a phone call...probably the most important call in the world.

MR. CZAROBSKI
The heads off the chickens, that's important. Phone calls don't pay the rent or make the food it takes when the big likes of you sits down to eat.

ZIGGY
Frank Leahy from Notre Dame, the big football coach is in town and he wants to see me. I might get a scholarship.

MR. CZAROBSKI
Scholarships!!! Talk...talk... cut...cut, that's what you should be doing.

The door to the shop opens and FRANK LEAHY comes in...

FRANK
Pardon me...

ZIGGY is flabbergasthed...

I'm Frank Leahy. Is this where I find Sygmond Czarobski...

ZIGGY
(out of his mind)
Me! Me!, that's me coach. I'm Ziggy...Sygmond Czarobski...And I'm a heck of a tackle.

MR. CZAROBSKI
A tackle...
(hands in the air)
So cut yet...

FRANK
Are you as mean and as tough as you look...

CONTINUED

FL - 127

199. CONTINUED

MR. CZAROBSKI
Mean, tough...the chicken's head he can't even cut off.

ZIGGY
(ignoring him)
Meaner and tougher...Is the Pope catholic?

FRANK
(shakes his hand)
Boy, you just got yourself a scholarship...I'll be in contact with you.

ZIGGY
Yes sir...

MR. CZAROBSKI
He should make contact with the meat ax, now he should.

FRANK
(laughs)
See you....

FRANK makes his exit, closing the door behind him. ZIGGY lets his cleaver fall to the chicken...a very bad cut...

MR. CZAROBSKI
Oiiiii....Lummox...the chicken... My beautiful chicken you've ruined... and we can't even eat it, it's not Kosher....

FADE TO:

200. INT. LEAHY LIVING ROOM - MEDIUM - NIGHT

[illegible] There is only one dim light in the far corner of the room. FLOSS is actually passed out on the living room sofa as FRANK comes in. He looks to her and the empty bottle on the coffee table near at hand....

DISSOLVE TO:

Recruiting Ziggy

This three page long scene comes from a couple lines in Williams' book, in which he interviews Zygmont (not Sygmond) "Ziggy" Peter Czarobski, who played tackle for Notre Dame from 1942 to 1947, with a break in the middle for military service. Czarobski later went on to play pro. He mentions in his interview that Leahy came to recruit him when he was working as a butcher, under his father, just like in the screenplay.

Wood takes advantage of this nugget to concoct a "colorful" scene, making sure to give Ziggy's dad plenty of lines in an ethnically stereotyped dialect that is not mentioned in the book. As cringe-inducing as this stuff is, it's at least an attempt by Wood to dramatize some interesting scenes in varied locations. It's oddly reminiscent of the scenes in Tim Burton's *Ed Wood* in which Johnny Depp, as Wood, visits Tor Johnson (George "The Animal" Steele) backstage at a wrestling match to recruit him for a movie, or when he meets with Donald McCoy (Rance Howard) in his meat packing plant.

FL - 128

201. EXT. TRAIN PLATFORM - MEDIUM - FRANK & FLOSS - DAY

A sign denotes the TWENTIETH CENTURY LIMITED.

FRANK
You will give my best to your folks?

FLOSS
Of course...Frank...I'm sorry about all this...my...drinking...

FRANK
Ahhh, Floss...

FLOSS
No let me finish. With you gone all the time and all those kids, and your mother isn't much help anymore...I just couldn't take it...I took to something else...

FRANK
I know honey. I know. I'm not blaming you. And don't worry about the kids. Ma is still able to take care of them. You just rest up, get some of that up-state New York fresh air, and you'll be fit as a fiddle sooner than you expect.

FLOSS
I hope so.

FRANK
I know so. A Leahy never lets anything beat him. Then you come right on back to us....

FLOSS
You'll write.

FRANK
You know how I am about letters... and all this recruiting...I'll see that Ma writes and tells you everything.
(questioning)
Floss...Are you sure that when Ma came to live with us, that that might have added, not lessened your burden?

CONTINUED

FL - 129

201. CONTINUED

FLOSS
Don't worry your head about things past...Your mother is a dear, sweet thing and tries so hard to be helpful and is a dream with the kids, but there are times when.....

She is cut off as the train rumbles into the station. They look to each other as the train slows then stops. FRANK kisses her quickly, and without another word she gets onto the train. FRANK hands her suitcase to a PORTER....

Then with the CAMERA MOVING with him FRANK moves far back toward the station proper, then again turns to look as the train starts off and soon is gone into the distance.

FADE TO:

202. INT. FRANK'S OFFICE - NOTRE DAME - MEDIUM CLOSE - NIGHT

FRANK is sitting at his desk, head in hands. He has a flask and a glass on the desk in front of him. He appears to be in some sort of pain, but is trying not to let it get him down. There is a knock on the door. FRANK quickly puts the flask and the glass into a desk drawer, then looks up.

FRANK
Come in.

MOOSE KRAUSE, one of his Assistant Coaches enters. He is taken aback by the ill look to his Coach.

MOOSE
Hi Coach...anything wrong?

FRANK
No Moose...No nothing...Just a little head ache...been working too hard...getting old I guess.

MOOSE
You'll never be old Coach...err, you know the way I mean that.

CONTINUED

Semi-Autobiographical?

Once again, the description of Frank alone at his desk could very well be Wood writing about himself:

"… sitting at his desk, head in hands. He has a flask and a glass on the desk in front of him. He appears to be in some sort of pain, but is trying not to let it get him down."

FL - 130

202. CONTINUED

FRANK
(attempted smile)
Sure, sure, Moose, I know. Did you make the arrangements?

MOOSE
Sure did! You're having lunch with the Lattner kid tomorrow.

FRANK
He's got potential that lad.

MOOSE
Yeah, but it's yakked around he's pretty well sold on Michigan. They've been biting his tail for a long time now.

FRANK
With his record I can't blame them. But I might have Notre Dame biting his tail off before lunch is over tomorrow.

DISSOLVE TO:

203. INT. RESTAURANT - CLOSE TWO - FRANK & LATTNER - DAY

They are in the middle of their lunch and LATTNER is a heavy eater...he is a big man.

FRANK
Sure I'm a hard Coach. I've got to be. Football is a hard game. I don't make it easy to play football for Notre Dame. You're good or you don't wear the uniform.

LATTNER
I've sure heard that alright.

FRANK
Well, that's about everything there is to tell. I'd like to have you play for Notre Dame and you can count on my personal attention for all of the next four years...

CONTINUED

FL - 131.

203. CONTINUED

LATTNER
Coach. You've been straight with me so I got to be straight with you. Coach Fritz Crisler over at Michigan has pretty well got me convinced to go with him... He's given me a pretty good deal.

FRANK
That's your decision Johnny... When will you finalize with Coach Crisler?

LATTNER
Couple of days from now.

FRANK
Seeing him personally?

LATTNER
Well...sure!

FRANK
Do me a favor?

LATTNER
If I can!

FRANK
I'm sure you can....
(sly)
Something has been troubling me. Ask him why his team is afraid to play Notre Dame.

LATTNER nearly spits his food out with the surprise move.

LATTNER
They are?

FRANK
(nods)
I figure they must be. We've been trying for five years to get them on our schedule...

LATTNER
Michigan is afraid to play you?

FRANK
It certainly looks that way. But you ask Coach Crisler and see.

CONTINUED

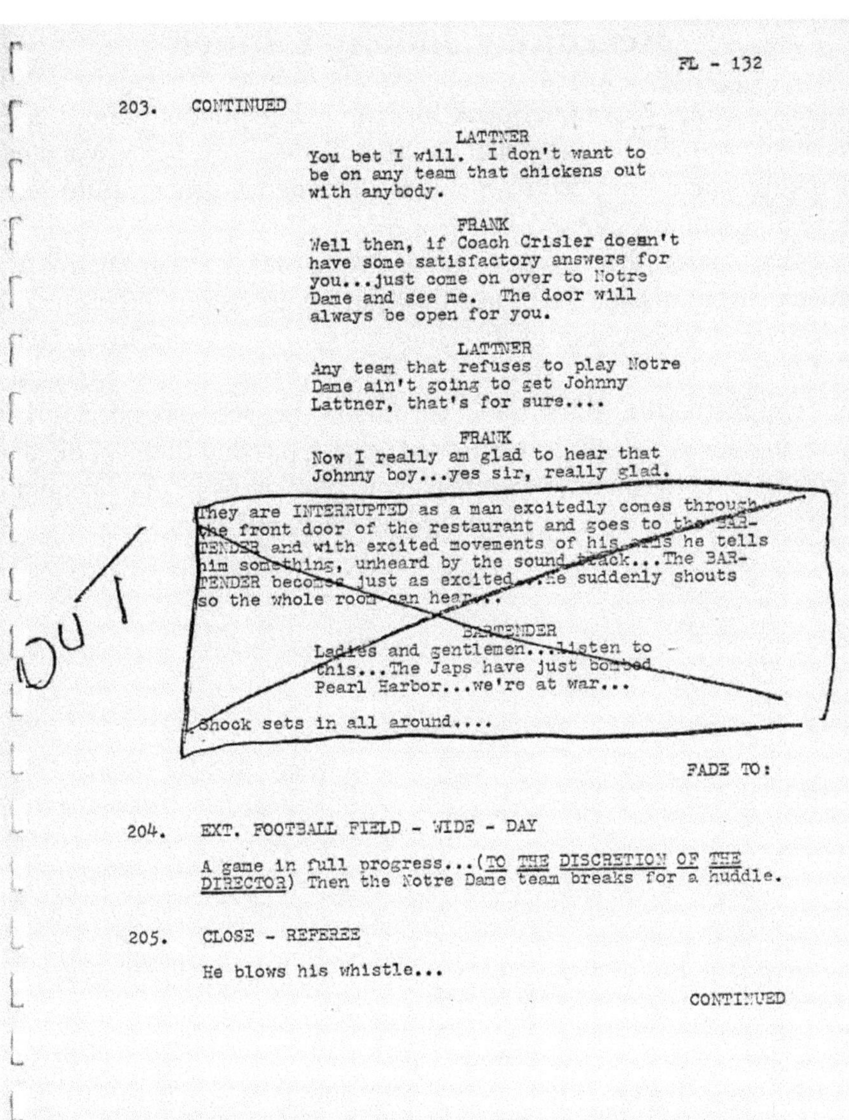

FL - 132

203. CONTINUED

LATTNER
You bet I will. I don't want to be on any team that chickens out with anybody.

FRANK
Well then, if Coach Crisler doesn't have some satisfactory answers for you...just come on over to Notre Dame and see me. The door will always be open for you.

LATTNER
Any team that refuses to play Notre Dame ain't going to get Johnny Lattner, that's for sure....

FRANK
Now I really am glad to hear that Johnny boy...yes sir, really glad.

They are INTERRUPTED as a man excitedly comes through the front door of the restaurant and goes to the BAR-TENDER and with excited movements of his arms he tells him something, unheard by the sound track...The BAR-TENDER becomes just as excited...he suddenly shouts so the whole room can hear...

BARTENDER
Ladies and gentlemen...listen to this...The Japs have just bombed Pearl Harbor...we're at war...

Shock sets in all around....

FADE TO:

204. EXT. FOOTBALL FIELD - WIDE - DAY

A game in full progress...(<u>TO THE DISCRETION OF THE DIRECTOR</u>) Then the Notre Dame team breaks for a huddle.

205. CLOSE - REFEREE

He blows his whistle...

CONTINUED

Recruiting Johnny Lattner

Johnny Lattner played halfback for Notre Dame under Frank Leahy from 1950 to 1953, so this scene is a little anachronistic as Wood has it taking place on December 7th, 1941, when Lattner would have been about nine years old.

That major discrepancy aside, Wood has Lattner mention a Coach Fritz Crissler "over at Michigan." Surprisingly, there *was* a Fritz Crissler coaching at the University of Michigan from 1938-1947.

The interesting thing about all this is this scene is not sourced from the book. Lattner is mentioned only in passing in the book, and Crissler is never mentioned, once again clueing us in that Wood did some research outside of just adapting Williams' book.

A Date Which Will Live in Infamy

There's a dramatic ending to this recruitment scene as the bartender announces that Pearl Harbor has been bombed, which is a significant moment in Leahy's life as it directly led to his military career, serving in the Navy from 1944 to 1945, some of that time actually at Pearl Harbor.

Of course the attack on Pearl Harbor famously took place on Sunday, December 7th, 1941 and the sale of alcohol in bars and restaurants on Sundays in Indiana was banned until 1973, so I'm not sure what the bartender's doing there in the first place.

Interestingly enough, this tag at the end of the scene is crossed out by hand with the note "OUT" on the screenplay – while there are many handwritten notes on this screenplay, this is the only scene selected for deletion. I wonder why?

FL - 133

205. CONTINUED

REFEREE
(calling)
Time!

206. CLOSE TWO - FRANK & MOOSE

On the sidelines.

FRANK
(exasperated)
Damn, I knew that would happen, and that's the last time out.

MOOSE
Yeah, the boys need more time.

FRANK looks down....

207. CLOSE - DOG - MASCOT...

Straining at his leash.

208. MEDIUM

FRANK quickly unhooks the dog. MOOSE is completely puzzled...

FRANK
Go get it boy....

The DOG makes a bee-line for....

209. ANGLED

...the ball which the REFEREE has just put down. The DOG attacks the ball to the amazement of all but the Notre Dame team who take advantage of the additional time while the REFEREEs chase about trying to get the ball away from the dog...all to the halarity of those not in on the know....

210. CLOSE TWO - FRANK & MOOSE

MOOSE, hands on hips looks from the field to FRANK.

CONTINUED

FL - 134

210. CONTINUED

MOOSE
I know you kidded about something like this, but I didn't think you'd use it...There's going to be hell to pay for sure.

FRANK
(stone faced)
Can I help it if the little mascot got loose...now tell me...can I help it?

MOOSE
(face breaks into broad grin)
You son of a gun...Yes, sir, you son of a gun....

MOOSE stops as a REFEREE comes in carrying the dog. He fairly jams it into FRANK's arms...

REFEREE
The rules of the game says eleven players...only eleven!!!

FRANK holds his most pious look as the REFEREE glares, then turns and skoots off onto the field again...MOOSE can hold it in no longer...he breaks up completely. FRANK'S pious look has turned skyward...hands folded in front of him...

FADE TO;

211. INT. FATHER JOHN CAVANAUGH'S OFFICE - MEDIUM - DAY

Just as FRANK enters and moves to a chair in front of CAVANAUGH'S desk...

CAVANAUGH
(pious)
(feigned)
That was some stunt you pulled out there this afternoon Frank.

FRANK
(feigned indignation)
Me? Why Father John, how could you think I would purposely do anything like that?

CONTINUED

FL - 135

211. CONTINUED

CAVANAUGH
No...no...of course not.

FRANK
Of course not...

And they both bellow with laughter....

Did you see the faces of those
Referees when that little dog
stole their ball....
(laugh)
Well, they needed something to
remember me by...my last game....

CAVANAUGH
(startled)
Last game? What are you talking
about?

FRANK
(nods)
At least for awhile.

CAVANAUGH
I...I...I don't know what to say.
I thought you were happy here....

FRANK
(cutting in)
Oh, don't get me wrong. The
happiest days of my life have
been here at Notre Dame...and
I hope to come back when...when
the War is over. I joined the
Navy earlier in the week. I'm
Commissioned a Lieutenant...
Floss is all well and she's back
home with me. Thought maybe I'd
take a little vacation this
time. We're pretty well off and
she can hire some help for Ma
and the kids...and I can use
a change too.

CAVANAUGH
Are you really up to it, Frank?

FRANK
Fit as a fiddle. Look John. My
boys are being taken in quicker
than I recruit them. I guess I
just want to be where my boys
are. Maybe they still need their

CONTINUED

FL - 136.

211. CONTINUED

FRANK (cont'd)
Coach with them to bring them to the touchdown line a winner.

CAVANAUGH
You know Frank Leahy, you're truly an amazingly, great man...

He gets up and moves to put his arm around FRANK'S shoulder...

You took the 1943 Coach of the Year last year, maybe in this 1944 year you'll come up with a different kind of Coach of the Year...God go with you...and protect you where-ever you go...and come back to us... soon...a winner....

212. EFFECTS

Bombs bursting...the war in general but mainly the Navy...and a spot shot of the Pacific Islands.... (TO THE DISCRETION OF THE DIRECTOR.) BERNIE'S NARRATION comes over. Also horseshoe game with Admiral Chester W. Nimitz.

BERNIE (Nar o.s.)
So Frank Laehy joined the war... One of his main duties was to scout out islands where our submarines would be safe from surprise air attacts when they had to lay over for one reason or another...He even got to pitch some horseshoes with Admiral Nimitz who was a great football fan and an even greater admirer of Frank Laehy, the Coach...

213. EXT. NOTRE DAME - FOOTBALL FIELD - LONG SHOT - HIGH - DAY

FRANK, still in uniform walks alone across the massive field. BERNIE'S NARRATION continues over.

BERNIE (Nar. o.s.)
The war ended for Frank in late

CONTINUED

God Loves a Terrier

Wood turns another brief anecdote from Leahy via Williams' book into a several page long scene. Leahy says in the book that they had a terrier on hand to repeatedly pull this stunt any time they were out of time outs but needed some extra minutes. When that was the case, Leahy would let the dog loose on the field and it would take the refs a few minutes to get it under control, during which planning for the next play could take place. In the book Leahy is careful to say this dog was a member of his team, not a mascot. Wood just calls it the team's mascot.

This is another example of Leahy cheating his way to success or "crying wolf" and this time even Father Cavanaugh doesn't seem to mind and even thinks it's funny. After all, it's only a game, right?

Leahy's War

Mostly left to the discretion of the director and covered in narration, Leahy joins the war effort just like Wood. Williams' book doesn't mention Leahy's job was to scout islands where submarines would be safe from air attacks, but it does go into his indoctrination at Princeton University, his supervision of athletic and recreational programs in Pearl Harbor, and stints at Midway, Majuro, Guam, Spain, Kwajalein, Tarawan and Myrtle. He brought with him a film called *The Highlights of the 1943 Notre Dame Season* and would exhibit it for the troops. He ended up back in Pearl Harbor.

The bit about playing horseshoes with Admiral Nimitz that Wood includes here is mentioned in Williams' book, though Wood goes above and beyond, making Nimitz a general football fan and specific Leahy fan.

When I saw that Leahy started his military career in Pearl Harbor in 1944 and spent some of it in the other Pacific Islands, I suddenly wondered if it was possible he and Wood had been in the same places at the same time. It almost seemed like a possibility when I learned that Wood was in Pearl Harbor May 6th of 1944. Unfortunately, that was the day he left, and although Leahy joined the military in 1944 and his first tour was in Pearl Harbor, he wasn't sworn in until May 19th, which means he arrived in Pearl Harbor after Wood left – ships passing in the night.

FL - 137

213. CONTINUED

BERNIE (Nar, o.s., cont'd)
1945...and he was still in uniform
as he reported back to Notre Dame.

A nother figure appears at the far end of the field just as FRANK attains that goal line. They are seen to shake hands.

214. CLOSE TWO - FIGURE - FRANK AND CAVANAUGH

As they shake hands warmly.

CAVANAUGH
Leave?

FRANK
Out!

CAVANAUGH
So soon?

FRANK
The Admiral was a football fan
and thought I was more use to
a team of football players than
to the Navy.

CAVANAUGH
The Navy's loss is our gain.

FRANK
But they wouldn't let me out
until after the Army Navy football
game...thought I might be some
kind of an influence if I stuck
my nose in...and there was another
very good reason. I've got four
kids now. Some of the Cleveland
boys want to lay thirty-five
thousand a year on me to Coach,
the Cleveland Leahys...

CAVANAUGH
(shocked)
Pro-football...Frank, you woulnd'nt.
You couldn't...

FRANK
(kicks turf)
Got to think of the family...

CONTINUED

FL - 138

214. CONTINUED

CAVANAUGH
But Fran,. You're the patron saint of Catholic football... You'll get your biggest reputation right here at Notre Dame. Frank, if not for me, for God sake for Our Lady...Look...As President I can authorize a bonus.

FRANK
(looks up)
Like what?

CAVANAUGH
Concessions and there are the programs.
(glances to the golden dome)
Frank, you've just got to come back to Our Lady.

He looks up to the Dome and his face brightens.

FRANK
That's all I wanted to hear... But you've got to ad in a fee from the parking lot concession!

Grabs his hand. Shakes it.

CAVANAUGH
You've got it Frank Leahy... Coach Extra <u>Ordinaire</u>...

FRANK grips the man's shoulder.

FRANK
And by the grace of Our Lady I'll win a hundred games in a row...And you can bet I'll do it. I recruited thrtee-three, twenty-one year old Freshmen while I was in the Pacific... all for Notre Dame...

CAVANAUGH
Why you old sea-dog...You highway robbing pirate...you were coming back to Notre Dame all the time. You held me up...and without a gun....

CONTINUED

FL - 139.

214. CONTINUED

FRANK
(grins - cocks his fingers like a pistol)
No gun maybe...but plenty of ammunition....

They laugh loudly and broadly...

Now I got to be on my way. I haven't even seen Floss and the kids yet. I came straight here.

CAVANAUGH
See you in the morning so we can go over final contract talks?

FRANK
The sooner the better Padre...

He starts off...

CAVANAUGH
So long...you pirate....

CAVANAUGH stands looking as his friend goes up the field.

FADE TO:

215. INT. LEAHY BASEMENT - WIDE - NIGHT

FRANK, FRANK III, FLOSS, & SUSAN are in volved in a mock football game...The purpose of the practice is to teach FRANK III his pivoting. FRANK runs the scrimmage with FLOSS centering and SUSAN playing the entire defensive.

FRANK
Let's go Frankie...Try a reverse pivot.

FRANKIE steps up behind his mother and calls the signals.

CONTINUED

FL - 140

215. CONTINUED

Upon the command of 42-A she snaps the ball and FRANKIE does the pivot his father wanted.

FRANK
Okay...Okay...Needs work, but that's pretty good for me not being around coaching you. You got to make that spin faster. You see the whole point is to fool the other guy...deception.., and the faster you twist that shoulder around, the easier it is for you to confuse the defense... at least temporarily and some times a few seconds is just long enough

(NOTE:- The kids are in mineature football uniforms, FRANK in sweatshirt and trousers...FLOSS, regular)

SUSAN
Can I try, Daddy?

FRANK
Oh I think you'd better stay defence for awhile. Frankie has got to know he's got big problems over there.

FRANKIE
Big problems? Susan?

FRANK
Now that's not the way to think about the thing. It's not Susan like she is there. It's what she represents. You see, she represents eleven men who have only one thing in mind...to get that ball away from you. That's why I say speed and deception is the most important objective.

FLOSS
Say Coach...would it be practical to have a dinner break?

CONTINUED

FL - 141

215. CONTINUED

FRANK
Just one more while he's wound up, Floss.

She Shruggs.

Okay Frankie, try 29-H.

FRANKIE goes behind FLOSS again, calls the signals to the 29-H, the ball is snapped...SUSAN waving her arms in attempting to block him which she does and he snaps the ball off to FRANK who is acting as the left halfback.

FRANK
Now that was good, really very good. The fake was good but the pitch out was sloppy yet. Arm came back too far before you let the ball go. Watch that. It's important. A defender could sneak up behind you and snatch the ball away from you before you knew what happened.
(pace change)
Okay...time's called. Upstairs and get washed for dinner...

SUSAN
Did I do good on defense Daddy?

FRANK
You bet you did, honey. You scared me worse than Army and Navy put together.

FLOSS is grinning, almost to laughter. She is happy.

SUSAN
(to Frankie)
See, Frankie...See...Daddy said I was a better defense than Army and Navy both.

The kids race off and up the stairs toward the main rooms above. FLOSS goes over and kisses FRANK then takes his arm lovingly as the CAMERA MOVES with them towards the steps.

CONTINUED

FL - 142

215. CONTINUED

FLOSS
It's nice to have you home Coach.

FRANK
You can't imagine how good it is
to be home...where I belong.

FLOSS
Was it terrible?

FRANK
War is war...there is never anything pleasant about war....
(pace change -
grin)
Suppose we could con the kids
into bed early tonight?

FLOSS
(coy)
That depends upon what you have
in mind, kind sir.

FRANK
Well...it's got nothing to do with
football...

The laugh and mount the stairs.

FADE TO:

216. EXT. FOOTBALL FIELD - GAME - NOTRE DAME & ARMY - WIDE -
DAY

Game, (TO THE DISCRETION OF THE DIRECTOR), and at some
point one of the PLAYERS misses a tackle.

217. MEDIUM - TO BENCH AREA

LUJAK jumps up from the bench, losing his blanket behind him. He is fuming with anger at the miss. FRANK
is near at hand.

LUJAK
(yells)
Livingston, you son-of-a-bitch!

CONTINUED

FL - 143

217. CONTINUED

FRANK spins on the man as he sits down again with the other players on the bench.

FRANK
Mr. Lujak, must I remind you we are representing Our Lady on this football field. There will be no profane language. What would your parents think if they heard such language, and after I promised them you'd be brought up in a good Catholic environment? I'm ashamed...truly ashamed...

FRANK looks back to the game.

218. MEDIUM - TO THE FIELD.

(TO THE DISCRETION OF THE DIRECTOR) as LIVINGSTON misses another tackle.

219. MEDIUM - TO FRANK & PLAYERS

on the bench. FRANK turns to them.

FRANK
Guys. It seems Mr. Lujack is right about Mr. Livingston.

WIPE DISSOLVE TO:

220. EXT. BLEECHERS - MEDIUM TWO - FRANK & CAVANAUGH - DAY

The two are slighly down in the dumps. FRANK has a rolled up program in his hand and he whisps at the step below him, then he looks up.

221. P.O.V. - SCOREBOARD

Showing NOTRE DAME "0" - ARMY "0"

222. MEDIUM TWO - FRANK & CAVANAUGH.

Frank sighs.

CONTINUED

FL - 144

222. CONTINUED

FRANK
Ties give me a pain where I sit down.

CAVANAUGH
We're not doing so bad Frank...
You promised a hundred and we're still undefeated after six...
There's only 94 to go.

FRANK stands up...preparing to go his own way.

Heard you've got some plans for tomorrow morning.

FRANK
Yeah...it's about time I kept a long standing promise.

WIPE DISSOLVE TO:

223. EXT. CEMETERY - ROCKNE GRAVESITE - WIDE - DAY

FRANK has several of his men with him and they are gathered around ROCKNE'S gravesite.

FRANK
A long time ago when I was in the Pacific I swore I'd make regular trips out here to Knute Rockne's grave for a little chat, in the hopes that some of his greatness would rub off on some of us...
And maybe each of us could offer up our own silent prayer in our own way.

He bows his head as do several of the others. But there are another group who wander off and the CAMERA PANS with them until they find another gravesite which they gather around.

224. MEDIUM GROUP -

The men look down to the new marker. It is for DANIEL CLANCY, the famous Notre Dame Basketball coach.

CONTINUED

FL - 145.

224. CONTINUED

KEAGAN
Daniel Clancy! What do you know about that.

LIMONT
Just about the greatest basketball coach Notre Dame ever had.

MILLER
White's still wet behind the ears. He's probably never heard of him.

WHITE
Ahhh, stick it where it will do the most good.

KEAGAN
Knock it off. Show some respect for Coach Clancy.

LIMONT
Sure...that's what we should do... We're out here, why not....

225. MEDIUM - FRANK

Looks up from his silent prayer. A frown crosses his features.

226. ANGLED

From behind FRANK to the other group at Clancy's grave.

FRANK
I can't believe it...
(hard-loud)
I can't believe that I'm actually seeing what I'm seeing. You guys get back over here. In basketball season you pray for the basketball coach...this is football season!!!

DISSOLVE TO:

Thoughts and Prayers

This anecdote about Leahy berating his players for praying at the wrong grave during the wrong sports season comes from Johnny Lujack in Williams' book. Lujack came from Pennsylvania and went on to play pro for Chicago. He was introduced to this story a few pages earlier, admonished by Leahy for cursing on the sidelines. Lujack's one of the more storied Notre Dame players of the era and it's a wonder he didn't get his own recruitment scene like Lattner and Czarobski, and just pops up unceremoniously on the sidelines instead.

FL - 146

227. EXT. FOOTBALL FIELD - EXTREME CLOSE - FRANK - DAY

FRANK is looking off to the game...the o.s. crowd is cheering wildly...the HEADLINES of sports pages flash into the scene...

SUPERIMPOSE...

"SIXTEEN STRAIGHT FOR NOTRE DAME"

"LEAHY 1947 COACH OF THE YEAR"

"CHALK UP 28 STRAIGHT FOR NOTRE DAME"

"CHARGES - NOTRE DAME UNFAIR"

"IRISH PULLING SHENANIGANS"

228. INT. HOSPITAL ROOM - MEDIUM - DAY

FLOSS is propped up in bed. She doesn't seem to be in any pain, but her leg is in a cast. FRANK bursts into the room. He looks quickly over the DOCTOR and a NURSE, then goes to FLOSS.

FRANK
Are you alright.?.what happened..?
what did you do? When....

The DOCTOR moves to him and tenderly takes him by the shoulders...

DOCTOR
(comforting)
You're wife will be alright Mr.
Leahy...she's broken her leg...

FLOSS
You know what that's like, you've
done it often enough...

FRANK
That's me. I got tough legs.
But your dainty little limbs...
You poor honey you...

FLOSS
It could have been worse.

CONTINUED

FL - 147

228. CONTINUED

FRANK
Worse? It could have been worse?
How?

FLOSS
It could have been Johnny Lujack!

FADE TO:

229. EXT. FOOTBALL FIELD - MEDIUM GROUP - HUDDLE - DAY

The Notre Dame team is in a huddle. Far in the background we can see the scoreboard with Notre Dame trailing at 25 to 27.

230. MEDIUM - TO BENCH AREA

FRANK paces back and forth in front of MOOSE.

FRANK
Less than a minute to go and
no more time out left.

MOOSE
Let the dog loose again.

FRANK
(frown)
That wouldn't work this time.
Oraco's gotta do it all by
himself.

231. MEDIUM GROUP - THE HUDDLE - UP ANGLE INTO FACES

ORACK is in charge.

ORACK
This time we're really up against
it fellas'...We've got to talk
to the coach. I mean I'm up the
creek without a paddle. On this
next play one of you faint...

Before a choice can be made the REFEREE calls them to the field and they immediately break and run off.

FL - 148

232. ~~[redacted]~~ WIDE - THE GAME

(TO THE DISCRETION OF THE DIRECTOR) to end the sequence with the ball is centered and just before the signal to snap both the ends fall to the ground in a feigned faint....

233. CLOSE - REFEREE

His mouth gapes then he blows the whistle...

234. CLOSE - FRANK

Suddenly laughs...The men run in. ORACO faces him.

FRANK
(seriously)
I'll never be able to convince anyone that this wasn't a simple broken play Steve.

ORACO
Right now Coach, I'm not so sure it was a good idea.

FRANK
We needed the time to talk.

235. MEDIUM CLOSE - CAVANAUGH

In the stands, looking off anxiously, worried toward the off scene FRANK and his PLAYERS talking.

236. MEDIUM GROUP - FEATURING FRANK

FRANK takes ORACO by the shoulder.

FRANK
So you've had a bad day so far. We all have bad days. But I know you can kick that ball better than anybody in those stands think you can.

ORACO
Sorry about all this Coach. I don't know what's gotten into

CONTINUED

FL - 149

236. CONTINUED

ORACO (cont'd)
me today. I should have made
all three of those field goals.
And I havent the lease excuse
for those points after...

FRANK
Just remember when the going gets
tough, we get tougher...Now get
back in there with ~~[illegible]~~ here TRIPUCKA
and show everybody just how
tough you are. Go get those
three points...Forget how you
were kicking...think how you're
going to kick now...

FRANK slaps the man on the back to send him on his way.

237. CLOSE - CAVANAUGH

Realizes that FRANK is sending ORACO in again.

CAVANAUGH
(Horrified)
Jesus Christ, Frank...NO!!! NOT ORACKO!!!

He then realizes what he has said and sinks back down to his seat, wishing there were walls all around him.

238. THE SCENE - FOR THE KICK

(To THE DISCRETION OF THE DIRECTOR) as ORACO makes good the kick.

239. MEDIUM - SCOREBOARD

The small window where the new number is to appear, the head of the SCOREKEEPER comes out and he is close to a micraphone....

SCOREKEEPER
God BLESS YOU STEVE ORACO!!!

The voice echoes over the loud speakers all over the [redacted] stadium.

FL - 150

240 CLOSE - FRANK

Snaps his head in the direction of the SCOREBOARD.

241. LONG SHOT - P.O.V.

There is no one there...only the change of figures showing Notre Dame ahead with 28...

242. CLOSE - FRANK

Slowly he lets his head drift up toward the heavens.

WIPE DISSOLVE TO:

243. INT. LOCKER ROOM - MEDIUM - LATER

Angling so that we can see the door leading into the locker room. FRANK is the only one there. He leans back in a chair in deep thought. His meditation is broken by two drunks, (fans) who are about to stagger by the door, but see FRANK and recognize him...

1st DRUNK
If it ain't old Leahy...Hey
them boys of yours did fine,
just fine out there today.

2nd DRUNK
But you don't take no credit for
that last kick by Oracko...No sir,
that was old Knute Rockne's
doin...We heard him shout down
from the sky "GOD BLESS YOU
STEVE ORACO". You don't never
mistake that voice once you
heard it...

FRANK
You think that way too, huh!

1st DRUNK
Wasn't nobody around that micraphone that could'a' done it...
(cocks eye)
Rockne alright.

FRANK gets up and moves to put his arms around each of their shoulders as he starts to walk off with them.

CONTINUED

FL - 151

243. CONTINUED

FRANK
Yes...somebody up there was looking over our shoulder's today...
(pace change)
Tell me. You boys got any of that fire water you've been drinking left?

1st DRUNK
We sure have...

2nd DRUNK
And what we ain't got, we can get...Be our guest Coach...

FRANK
Don't mind if I do boys...

FADE TO:

244. EXT. FRANK'S FIRE STATION OFFICE - WIDE - ESTABLISHING - NIGHT

One of the windows is lighted with the flickering lamp of a projector...

DISSOLVE THROUGH:

245. INT. FRANK'S OFFICE - MEDIUM - PAN - NIGHT

FRANK is watching football footage on the screen. He occassionally looks to his watch, then above the clatter of the projector gears he hears the small tinkling of a bell. His eyes brighten. He grabs up his jacket and slips it on, then leaving the projector running he makes his way to the fire pole, CAMERA PANNING, and he slides down it.

247. EXT. THE FIRE STATION OFFICE - MEDIUM - PAN - NIGHT

FRANK comes out of the fire station and the CAMERA PANS him across to a lovely girl wearing an angora slip-over sweater and short skirt. She stands near a bicycle.

CONTINUED

God Bless You, Stephen Oracko

This rare bit of in-game business is not mentioned in Williams' book, though it is a popular enough Notre Dame story to be mentioned elsewhere, once again proving Wood looked into more than just his direct source material for this job. Whoever corrected these pages was also familiar with the story, fixing the spelling of Oracko's name, fixing the score of the game and replacing Lujack's name with Tripucka – probably Williams himself.

Wood does combine two different stories here, though. The fainting trick was used by Notre Dame most famously in a 1953 game – Oracko's miraculous field goal kick was in 1948. So, the patented "crying wolf" part of this story actually comes from later in Leahy's career. This time Wood has one of Leahy's players decide to cry wolf all on his own, showing that Leahy's tactics are rubbing off on his players, for better or worse.

The end of the sequence, where the scorekeeper calls out "God bless you, Stephen Oracko!" from the scoreboard and is mistaken by the crowd for the ghost of Knute Rockne is a legitimate part of the story – however, in real life, it was not the scorekeeper who called it out, but Leahy's assistant, McArdle, who watched games from behind the scoreboard for a better vantage point on the opposing team.

When the Going Gets Tough…

The most famous quote attributed to Frank Leahy is, "When the going gets tough, let the tough get going," which is part of a poem called "Don't Quit." In Williams' book, Leahy gives credit to getting the phrase from the poem, but it's left as somewhat of a mystery as to who originally wrote it, and even the Internet seems confused as to who did – a few names are attributed to it, but nothing concrete.

Wood includes the quote here, but alters it a bit to "…when the going gets tough, we get tougher…"

FL - 152.

247. CONTINUED

When she sees FRANK she stands tall and he takes her in his arms for a heated kiss. He indicates the soft fur of her sweater as they break.

FRANK
You look and feel like a little bunny rabbit, Cindy.

CINDY
All soft, just for you...

FRANK
Ummmmmmm...

He starts to kiss her again...but the sound of footsteps approaching causes them to grab the bike and duck into the thick brush behind them. TWO PRIESTS come into the scene and pause momentarily to look up at the flickering light of FRANK's window.

1st PRIEST
Will you look at that. The Saint's be praised. I've never known a man to work as hard as Coach Leahy...

2nd PRIEST
He'll kill himself with work yet...

Then they walk out of the scene...a light giggle is heard from the bushes.

FADE TO:

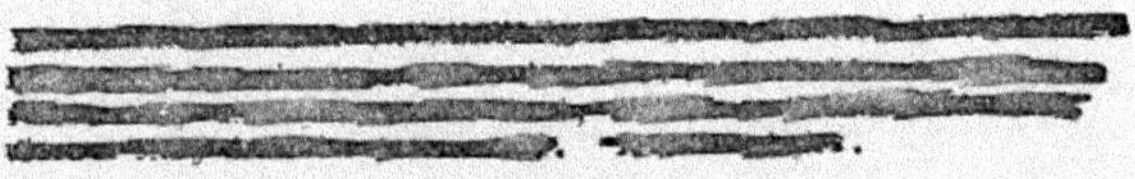

Angora Fever

Perhaps the single most exciting scene for Ed Wood fans begins on page 151 and ends on page 152 as Wood's favorite fabric, angora, makes its trademark appearance. That was one of the biggest questions on my mind when I first got hold of this screenplay – would Wood be able to fit his signature reference to angora into a football screenplay? The answer is, of course.

The sequence starts out confusingly enough, for casual readers, as it unceremoniously introduces Leahy's "fire station office" without explanation. To those uninitiated to Notre Dame lore, it might seem at first odd that Notre Dame has a fire station on campus at all and second even more strange that their football coach both worked and slept there.

This is mentioned in Williams' book, by Czarobski, who says Leahy slept on an old army cot in the fire station during the week, watching game film late into the night, working eighteen hour days, and then commuted back home to his wife and family on the weekends, a 50 minute drive. No judgment is ever passed on this fact, but Williams' book mentions Floss' absence from Notre Dame life multiple times, as if intending to imply something.

Wood seemingly interprets this to mean that Leahy's womanizing ways continued even into his marriage, in this throwaway scene of joyous infidelity. Again, Leahy is presented as a cheater who never gets caught and only prospers – this time, cheating on his wife. By this point of the screenplay, Floss has conquered her alcoholic demons, but this dalliance is strange in a narrative that has only built up the relationship between Leahy and Floss as a positive one. Normally, one might portray a rocky or unfulfilling relationship to justify the extramarital actions of the spouse. Not here. It's neither played as positive or negative. It's just another thing that happens.

But let's get to the angora, shall we? First, it's important to note the movies return to the scene again, starting this sequence with "the flickering lamp of a projector." Leahy's watching game footage, per Williams' book, waiting for some kind of signal – when it comes in the form of a tinkling bicycle bell, he jumps up with joy and literally slides down a fire pole to get to his mistress, "a lovely girl wearing an angora slip-over sweater and short skirt." Wood even mentions the "soft fur of her sweater" and includes dialogue about it.

Then, just to cap things off, Wood gives Leahy a line of dialogue directly out of the inter-titles of the pornographic loops he had recently written and directed, a nice, big, long "Ummmmmmm…" That's seven Ms, folks.

The following scene is blacked out, whether by Wood, Williams or someone else, and since it follows such a remarkably Woodian moment, it is tempting to imagine it continues the short saga of Cindy and her angora. Unfortunately, we may never know. Notice, there's no discretion to the Director when it comes to women's clothing choices.

Again, imagine Williams is telling this story to his son. Sheesh.

248. CONTINUED

CAVANAUGH
You've got to bend a little Frank.
You've got to see something of
their way. Look! You know it as
well as I. Just about everybody
is dropping us from their schedules.
Army, Navy...everybody. You've won
thirty-nine games in a row. They're
sick and tired of "having the crap"
kicked out of 'em.

FRANK
The Board Members should be screaming
"HURRAY FOR LEAHY"
(toss off)
Maybe I should have thrown a
couple of games.

CAVANAUGH
I wouldn't go that far....
(pace change -
official)
The press criticizms are bad...
Very bad...The brass want to deemphasize football...

FRANK
Deemphasize Leahy, you mean.

CAVANAUGH
(ignors him)
From now on you'll do your recuriting
by mail instead of personal contact
as you have been doing, and instead of thirty-three scholarships
there will be only eighteen.

FRANK
(whistles)
Eighteen?...and how do I recognize
talent over the phone?

CAVANAUGH
It's out of my hands Frank. This
shake-up in the administration
has me tredding lightly. When
Father Hesburgh, you just met,
became vice-president of vice-
presidents he took most of my
powers with the job.

CONTINUED

FL - 154

248. CONTINUED

FRANK
I know it's not your fault John.

CAVANAUGH
You must admit you are becoming completely unpredicitible.

FRANK
I've got to ride with the tide. If something needs changing on the spot to win, then I'm going to make that change.

CAVANAUGH
Like you're doing with the "T" formation. When you switched from the Notre Dame Shift to the "T" formation the alums thought you'd gone off your rocker...But I backed you. So what's with this reverse now... switching back again?

FRANK doesn't answer.

Oh, I know, even if they don't. The moment we move, just before we wait our second-and-two-tenths, THEY, think it's a "T" play and will be drawn off-side and get twenty yards! That's part of the alumni's complaint...so don't do it anymore.

FRANK
(exasperated)
What the hell have they got to complain about when we get twenty yards everytime we pull it?

CAVANAUGH
That's just the point. Pulling things. Notre Dame players and coaches are not supposed to go around, pulling things.

FRANK
There's nothing illegal about what I do.

CONTINUED

FL - 155

248. CONTINUED

CAVANAUGH
(hard)
Legality is not the issue.

FRANK
These things are used against us.

CAVANAUGH
You simply don't want to understand.

FRANK
You're the one who doesn;t understand...you and that bunch who just left here...this is MY TEAM!

CAVANAUGH
It's Notre Dame's team. And the glory of Notre Dame will be here long after all of us are gone

FRANK
(ignoring)
I have an obligation to make them win...

CAVANAUGH
You have an obligation to this University also...
(pointedly)
Frank, you're not to use that sucker shift again...if you do...
(suddenly - quietly)
...I'll have to ask for your resignation.

FRANK storms to his feet. He quickly goes to the door.

FRANK
You may already have asked for it!

He goes out and slams the door behind him. CAVANAUGH is very troubled about what he has had to do.

FADE TO:

249. INT. LEAHY'S OFFICE - MEDIUM - NIGHT

FRANK sits in front of one of the early model television

CONTINUED

FL - 156

249. CONTINUED

sets...a small picture with a large magnifying bulb in front. There is the distorted picture of FATHER JOHN CAVANAUGH talking.

CAVANAUGH
(on T.V.)
The condition of the loser is not improved in the estimation of the public by criticizing the winner. The American people who worship a winner so long as he wins honestly, according to the rules, are not easily led by such accusations. We at Notre Dame make no apology about wanting winners. We shall always want Notre Dame to play to win!..just as long as there is a Notre Dame. As to the criticism of Coach Leahy's methods...Tell me. Is a man to be criticized because of his ability to condition his team? His imagination in devising an affective running and passing game, for his uncommon power to teach fundamentals; for his extraordinary success in holding a team up to a high standard of perfection week after week? I think not. Instead, I feel Frank Leahy deserves unqualified credit for his coaching record.
(pace change)
Confidentially, and speaking just among ourselves, much of the distress about Frank Leahy is due to the fact that he is admittedly the most able football coach in the nation.

There is loud applause on the television from an unseen audience. FRANK gets up from his chair, puts down the glass of burbon he has been drinking and moves to turn off the set. A broad, pleased grin crosses his features.

FRANK
There you go again, you old bastard... Sticking your neck out for me...and way out it is...So, okay, I'll play some more football for you...

Sits down with the bourbon again...

For awhile longer, any way...

FADE TO:

Ethics

In this sequence, Leahy is finally taken to task for playing fast and loose with the rules. We can safely assume the action has moved into the 50s here, as Reverend Theodore Hesburgh, president of Notre Dame from 1952 to 1987, enters the scene. From Leahy's point of view, Hesburgh is putting ethical restraints on Notre Dame that other schools don't have to follow, thus putting them at a disadvantage and positioning Hesburgh as a bit of a bad guy in this screenplay.

In real life, Hesburgh was a champion of civil rights, to the point of hobnobbing with the likes of Dr. Martin Luther King, Jr. and serving as the Chair of the United States Commission on Civil Rights from 1969 to 1972. Wood's screenplay positions him as moving the university away from football – that is one way of looking at it, but another is that Hesburgh was responsible for turning Notre Dame into the nationally respected institution of higher education that it is today.

Of course, Wood's right not to get into all this when he's writing a screenplay about the legend of Frank Leahy, but it's interesting to note the position the screenplay is taking – position a progressive guy like Hesburgh as an old fuddy duddy and a liar and a cheat like Leahy as a revolutionary hero.

To heighten the drama, Leahy even gets into a possibly career ending argument with Cavanaugh – only for Cavanaugh to come around in the end.

FL - 157

250. EXT. FOOTBALL FIELD - WIDE - NOTRE DAME vs GEORGIA TECH - DAY

Game(to the discretion of the director).

251. CLOSE - BENCH

FRANK is obviously ill. He is ashen and has his coat bundled tightly about him. FATHER CAVANAUGH comes in close to him at the PLAYER'S Bench.

CAVANAUGH
You don't look so good Frank.
Your eyes are miserable.

FRANK
You think they're bad from that side, you should see them from this side...It's been more than a month...just can't seem to get with it...pain...weak... shaking all over.

CAVANAUGH indicates the game.

CAVANAUGH
Why don't you bust out? The game is in the bag. The boy's don't need you anymore today...Less than two minutes.

FRANK
The boys always need me...right up until the gun goes off.

A particular play grabs his attention and he jumps to his feet with full power.

(screams)
Damn it Miller, you know better than that....

And FRANK LEAHY is gripped with a sudden, tremendous pain which screws up his face. He doubles up and grabs at his lower guts. FATHER JOHN CAVANAUGH tries to grab him, but FRANK falls to the ground. It would appear that he is near death in the silence of sound and movement to his body. Others rush in to his side.

WIPE DISSOLVE TO:

FL - 158

252. INT. LOCKER ROOM - MEDIUM GROUP - DAY

FRANK is stretched out on a rub-down table. He is as still as death. The DOCTOR is still going over his chest, the shirt has been open. CAVANAUGH stands close at hand. MOOSE, the Assistant Coach is also there. The DOCTOR Stands up.

CAVANAUGH
What's the virdict Doctor, and don't give me your usual "Bad enough" observation.

DOCTOR
(gravely)
Not this time Father...
(to Moose)
You'd better notify Mrs. Leahy.

CAVANAUGH
Good Lord!
(crosses himself)

DOCTOR
(looks to him)
His heart is so weak I can hardly detect it. My considered opinion... He'll never make the hospital. I think...I think Father you'd better administer the last rites.

CAVANAUGH
You...you can't mean it.

DOCTOR
(shakes head)
I wish I didn't...

He turns to the door and goes out into the crowd of reporters who ad-lib their questions...the door closes them out. FATHER CAVANAUGH prepares to give FRANK the last rites.

253. INT. HALLWAY - TO LOCKER ROOM - WIDE - DAY

Crowded with reporters excitedly asking their questions. The DOCTOR holds up his hands for silence...at the same time an ELDERLY JANITOR who has been nipping from his hip bottle comes up to stand next to the door and to the DOCTOR. He tries focusing his eyes...What has happened to FRANK filters through to him however.

CONTINUED

FL - 159

253. CONTINUED

DOCTOR
We'll make a formal statement
in due course gentlemen, but
for your early editions, Coach
Leahy is...Father John Cavanaugh
is administering the last rites
at this very moment. It is
my considered opinion that the
Coach cannot last out the hour...

CAVANAUGH comes out. His face is grave. The REPORTERS hop all over him. However, CAVANAUGH has left the door slightly adjar. The JANITOR sneaks a look inside, then unseen by the others who are paying him no attention, he goes in and closes the door behind him.

254. INT. LOCKER ROOM - MEDIUM - DAY

The JANITOR swipes off his cap and tucks it under his arm. He walks to FRANK and looks down at the death-like body. A tear comes to the old man's eyes.

JANITOR
Sure gonna' miss you around here
Coach. Missed old Knute when he
was gone, and there ain't been
nobody like him 'round here 'till
you came along.

The man has a very thick Irish brogue, and in his almost drunken state it is even thicker.

But sure 'tain't fittin' for a
big Irish lad like you to go up
there to join Saint Peter and
Knute without the least little
smell of the Irish on your lips.

He takes the flask from his hip pocket, uncorcks it and forces some between FRANK'S lips and down into his throat. FRANK snaps up on the table as if an electrical shock of some magnitude has been sent through his body.

FRANK
(screams)
GOOD GOD!!! WHAT THE HELL WAS
THAT ROT GUT?

CONTINUED

FL - 160

254. CONTINUED

The door bursts open and the DOCTOR and CAVANAUGH race in..."What's going on?" "What Happened?" "Frank!" "Good God"... The DOCTOR races across to FRANK, with CAVANAUGH hot on his heels. The JANITOR is still in his position on the other side of the table. The DOCTOR eases FRANK back to the table and starts going over him with his stethoscope...CAVANAUGH looks to the JANITOR.

CAVANAUGH
What happened here?

JANITOR
The Coach made a remarkable
recovery, that he did...

FADE TO:

255. INT. HOSPITAL ROOM - MEDIUM - DAY

FLOSS is arranging some flowers, and FRANK propped up in bed, looking much better and more like his old self is on the telephone. It is apparent he's been on the phone for some time.

FRANK
Okay Moose...take out Miller and
send in Oracko...don't argue
with me...send in Oracko and play
the 24-A, it's an old one but
it should work...
(pause)
Wait a minute now...

He checks some hand drawn charts in front of him...makes a new "X" for another position...

Flag down White, he's going too
fast....
(pause)
That's my boys...Kick it Oracko...
Scream at him Moose...tell him
it's for the old coach, just
like he did when our backs were
to the wall that other time....
(pause - sighs -
hangs up phone)
They can't lose!!!

He lays back.

CONTINUED

Alternative Medicine

Of course Leahy's 1953 mid-game collapse is covered in the main body of Williams' book, but this sequence involving the janitor that Wood focuses on is only in the original version – the 2009 re-printing removes this anecdote, originally included in a section called "Interesting Angles, Statistics and Glimpses." While most of the stories in the rest of the book either come from interviews with Leahy himself, or those who knew him, this anecdote is unattributed by Williams to anyone.

In the book, it plays out basically as it does in Wood's screenplay; however, Wood made sure to give the janitor plenty of ethnically stereotyped dialogue, positioning him as almost a magical leprechaun, and naming him Patrick. Another screenwriter might have planted the character of the magical janitor a little bit earlier and had him appear throughout for this payoff, but not Wood.

It's tempting to assume the healing power of alcohol comes directly from Wood's imagination, but it is true to Williams' book. Wood does change Williams' "rock-gut" to "rot-gut", however.

FL - 161

255. CONTINUED

FLOSS
I'd never believe it!

FRANK
What?

FLOSS
That you could actually side-line coach your team from a hospital bed.

FRANK
I know every play...I know where they are every second...right here on my charts...
(taps charts)
...can't miss...a little expensive though....

FLOSS
Okay, so now your games are all played until next weekend. How about laying back and getting some rest...

FRANK
I gotta keep with them when they practice as well as when they play.

FLOSS
Well they don't even practice until Monday...lay back. You've got to rest. Look Frank Leahy. You've had a bad time of it. When they start giving you your last rites, that should mean something to you.

FRANK
It does...Floss. What would you think if I really did retire?

FLOSS
I'd be the happiest woman in the whole world...and the kids would love it...they're growing fast. Look how big Frankie is...teens almost gone and the others are catching up to him...

CONTINUED

FL - 162

255. CONTINUED

FRANK
Think you could stand having me around the house all the time?

FLOSS
I could...but knowing you, you wouldn't be around the house very much. You'd find something to do. I only hope it's away from football fields.

FRANK
This leukemia stuff keeps draining my strength...I won't be running many more football fields, side-line or otherwise. You know I have to have four pints of blood a month from now on...

FLOSS
I know...
(sadly)

FRANK
They can't cure the damned thing... but they can arrest it and keep that terrible pain down. I don't like that pain...No...I'll finish out the season...then look for something else. A lot of people want me for speeches... lot of youth organizations too... want me to keep the kids clean and healthy...
(light laugh)
Look who's going to talk about health...the blind leading the blind...

FLOSS
You'll live to be a hundred and two.

FRANK
I'll kind of miss my beer and the taste of the old Irish....
(suddenly)
Say did we ever send that case of Irish whiskey to old Patrick the Janitor who pulled me through?

CONTINUED

FL - 163

255. CONTINUED

FLOSS
(sigh)
Yes...Yes. You've asked me that question every day for the month you've been here...everytime you think about the fact you can never touch it again...

FRANK
It's not that I forget...
(grins)
It's just that I'm forgetful...

256. EXT. FOOTBALL FIELD - WIDE - DAY - MONTAGE

A MONTAGE of football games, INTERCUTTING FRANK with his Assistant coaches...(TO THE DISCRETION OF THE DIRECTOR).

BERNIE (o.s.)(Narration)
Bernie didn't quit that season... and his health suffered more and more...there were more trips to the hospital. The Father's forced him to take vacations...short short vacations...but he always returned...Then.

257. INT. DOCTOR'S OFFICE - CLOSE TWO - FRANK & DOCTOR - DAY

The DOCTOR has just finished examining FRANK who is sitting up on the metal operating table.

FRANK
Okay...give it to me straight Doc...plain and simple.

DOCTOR
(shakes head)
Okay...plain and simple Frank... You either stop coaching foot-ball or you stop living...

WIPE DISSOLVE TO:

258. INT. AUDITORIUM - NOTRE DAME - EXTREME WIDE - DAY

FRANK with many of the other IMPORTANTS of the University including CAVANAUGH are on the stage. FRANK is at the speakers podium...tears of sorry will river down his

CONTINUED

FL - 164

258. CONTINUED

cheeks from emotion at points (TO THE DISCRETION OF THE DIRECTOR.) In the background FATHER JOHN CAVANAUGH can also be seen to dab at his eyes a time or two, attempting not to show his emotions to anyone else. There will be INTERCUTS in CLOSE & MEDIUM CLOSE of FRANK, CAVANAUGH, FATHER HESBURGH, and many of the players such as MOOSE, LUJACK, ZIGGY, LATTINER, ETC., through out the speech, (TO THE DISCRETION OF THE DIRECTOR.) Various forms of emotions have taken over the spirit of each.

FRANK

I suppose you know what this assembly is all about...I know how word travels on this campus...

There is a light laugh from the nervous atendees.

Recently, well last season, I thought I was dying. You all knew about that...during the Georga Tech game...Well I recovered, or I thought I had. I finished out that season and I have finished this one, but now I *know* this has been my last season of football. Next year I'm going out into the world of business...There are other businesses around other than football, you know...

Again very light, nervous laughter from the audience.

Therefore this occasion of my leaving the coaching of football seems the perfect time to answer some criticisms leveled at our school...*Me* in particular! Feigned injuries have been a part of football since Walter Camp invented the first down, more than seventy years ago. Southern Methodist has used it against us, and so has Oklahoma, Pittsburgh, Cal-Tech, Georgia Tech...you name them and they've all used that tactic. "Be sure", Knute Rockne used to tell me, "that the man who fakes the injury has a most capable replacement. It seems to me that the feigned

CONTINUED

FL - 165

258. CONTINUED

FRANK (Cont'd)
injury controversy, just like the Shift controversy was caused not by what was done, but by who did it and how successfully. And another thing. Much as I hate to lose I never squealed and I have never alibied. Rock taught me that and I never forgot it. I am handling my own illness in the same way. I don't plan to lose however. ...but after many years of reocurring illness and that time when the good Father John performed the last rites over me I have made my decision. My health is such presently that I can no longer continue coaching, therefore as of tomorrow morning, January 31st, in this year of our Lord 1954, I am resigning as Head Coach of Notre Dame... My heart will always be with Notre Dame and my heart will suffer in what I must do. But I leave knowing that others will carry on our noble tradition as I have tried so desperately to do....

LONG FADE TO:

259. MONTAGE OF SCENES

Office doors with the names of corporations FRANK becomes associated with in the business world...His name is always prominent under the name of the company as PRESIDENT or VICE PRESIDENT... "CANTEEN CORPORATION OF AMERICA" - - "PACIFIC COAST TITLE INSURANCE COMPANY" - A shot of FRANK at a microphone - HAMILTON OIL AND GAS COMPANY" - (NOTE:- must be last "LEAHY-WOLFSON INSURANCE AND BONDING COMPANY") FRANK broadcasting on television.

BERNIE (NAR. O.S.)
If Frank were alive today he would be the first to tell you that he was the worlds worst business man... He was good at the TV. commentary for Mayor Daly of Chicago, but it didn't last long enough to make it all worthwhile.

CONTINUED

A Petty Resignation Speech

In this sequence, Leahy resigns as Notre Dame coach due to health concerns, and what starts out as an emotional moment transforms quickly into a petty and defensive speech in which Leahy takes the chance to defend his gimmicky way of skirting the rules of football. I checked one contemporary newspaper report at the time about his resignation, and it did not mention this aspect, so perhaps Leahy's real-life speech was a little less defensive, though Williams' book does mention that while Leahy was happy with most of the press surrounding his resignation, he was unhappy with one report that criticized his use of fake injuries. In Williams' book, Leahy claims he offered a rebuttal to this criticism in an article he wrote for *Look* magazine, which, based on what Leahy says about it, sounds like it covers much of the same material as Wood's Leahy speech here.

A quick Google search reveals Leahy *did* write an article for the March 23rd, 1954 issue of *Look* magazine called, "Farewell to Notre Dame." Audrey Hepburn was featured on the cover as Actress of the Year.

FL - 166

259. CONTINUED

BERNIE (cont'd)
(O.S. Narration)
He did enjoy working for Pat O'Malley
And the Canteen Corporation of America,
but all the others into which he
sunk as much as two hundred thousand
dollars were doomed to failure....

260. INT. FOYER - FANCY OFFICE - MEDIUM - DAY

FRANK, well dressed in a neat business suit comes into the foyer of the LEAHY-WOLFSON INSURANCE AND BONDING COMPANY. He indicates the outside to the secretary.

FRANK
What's all those big expensive
cars doing out in the parking
lot?

SECRETARY
Board meeting Mr. Leahy.

FRANK
Why in hell wasn't I informed.
Where's Lou?
(points to board
room)
In there?

SECRETARY
He left strict orders that he
was not to be disturbed...<u>no</u>
<u>one</u> is to be admitted.

FRANK
(hot)
Well damn it, I'm not one of
the <u>no</u> <u>ones</u>...I'm a partner.

He stomps across the room and throws open the door and enters the board room.

261. INT. BOARD ROOM - WIDE - DAY

LOU WOLFSON is at the head of the table and several other business men are seated around the table.

CONTINUED

FL - 167

261. CONTINUED

LOU
Well, Frank...Gentlemen, my
partner, Frank Leahy...

FRANK seems to have expected something else. But he is determined to find out why he was not invited.

FRANK
Alright Lou...let's talk.

LOU
(takes him by
the arm)
Sure...of course Frank...Will
you excuse us a moment gentlemen...
(leads him back
through door)
Out here, Frank...
(buttering)
You look a little tired....

262. INT. SECRETARY'S OFFICE - CLOSE TWO - FRANK & LOU - DAY

LOU closes the door behind them and they stand just outside of the door. LOU has continued his conversation already started in the board room.

LOU (continuing)
...You got to watch yourself.
You know you're getting up
around Rock's age...

FRANK
I don't fly...What's with you
Lou...I give you my dough...I
want to learn the business and
I'm left out of everything...
I always thought you liked
me Lou.

LOU
I do...I do...You must know
that Frank.

FRANK
Okay, then why is it I never
set in on the board meetings?

CONTINUED

FL - 168

262. CONTINUED

LOU
I just didn't want to trouble you Frank...your health and all...You need the rest. I can handle the business for both of us...I mean these things...they concern things that are far over your head...at least until you learn the game... You know how bad you are at numbers...

FRANK
How am I going to learn a God damn thing when I'm kept out of it all all the time? I don't feel I'm contributing anything to the business...and I tell you one big fact Lou...
(hard)
The people I try to sell say, "We believe in you, Frank, but we think that dirty Kike so-and-so is just using your fine Irish Catholic name." How about that Lou?

LOU
Son's-a-bitches. You know I mean right by you. Don't worry about what people say? People gotta' talk, and they'd rather slander than face facts...
(promoting)
Now...there's another position I've been considering for you.
(confidential)
Now don't let this get around because some of the board members aren't in on it yet. But I want you to come over to the parent organizztion as vice-president in charge of trade relations... Forty-thosand a year...hew does that grab you? Plenty of goodies for Floss and the kids...how many now?

FRANK
Eight...

CONTINUED

FL - 169

262. CONTINUED

LOU
(feigned surprise)
Eight...
(light laugh)
Who says you're in ill health?

LOU slaps FRANK a heafty one on the shoulder. FRANK doesn't like it, but he takes it.

And this part I can guarantee. You know when I guarantee something I keep my word. You've learned that over the past two years, I'm sure...Through stock manipulation I'll get you an easy one hundred thousand a year. All I have to do is tell you when to get in and when to get out...just listen to me... Trust me...

FRANK
Okay...I trust you....

263. INT. COURT ROOM - WIDE - DAY

FRANK and LOU with their ATTORNIES are at one table and the COMMISSION ATTORNIES are at the other.

BERNIE (o.s. - Narration)
Frank might have trusted him, but the Securities Commission didn't and the company was taken to court. It was proved how Frank was dupped and he had all the charges dismissed. Lou went to prison...

DISSOLVE TO:

264. INT. FATHER JOHN CAVANAUGH'S OFFICE - MEDIUM TWO - FRANK & CAVANAUGH - DAY

FRANK sits in the chair across from JOHN that he had sat in many a time during his coaching days.

CONTINUED

All Business

Wood handles Leahy's post-coaching-career foray into the world of business in a quick narrated montage and a few pages covering his encounter with Lou Wolfson. According to Wood's screenplay, though Wolfson got into legal trouble for whatever he was into, Leahy was merely a patsy and was left off the hook.

In Leahy's telling in the Williams book, Leahy makes it sound like Wolfson was up to some insider trading that Leahy declined to participate in. However, Leahy doesn't cite the insider trading as the reason he didn't continue with Wolfson. He says the main two reasons it didn't work out was because Wolfson excluded him from important meetings, which hurt his feelings, and because he didn't like the way he saw an elderly steel mill manager laid off from his job.

Either way, both Williams' book and Wood's screenplay have Leahy tangentially involved in something that's not on the up and up – only as usual, it's not his fault, and he gets away with it.

Wolfson was a self-made millionaire and financier who created the concept of the hostile takeover and ran afoul of the law when he was accused of "fraudulent and manipulative practices" which would be the situation Leahy was involved in (apparently indirectly). Later, he was convicted of selling unregistered shares and obstruction of justice. His early life paralleled Leahy's a little, as he was a boxer in his teens and played football in college.

Wolfson wasn't all bad, though. After a terrible experience in prison, he became a prison reform advocate.

Wood's version of the story puts an incredibly ugly epithet in Leahy's mouth and no one came along and crossed it off, so I guess they were fine with that being part of the "legend."

FL - 170

264. CONTINUED

CAVANAUGH
You can imagine the pleasant surprise it was for me when you called and said you were in South Bend. I've arranged dinner for us at your favorite restaurant in town.

FRANK
That's great. It'll be like old times.

FRANK tries to be happy about the reunion, but CAVANAUGH realizes quickly that he is troubled...and the trouble makes FRANK'S illness look even greater.

CAVANAUGH
You got troubles Frank?

FRANK
Have I got troubles...coming out of my ears, John.

CAVANAUGH
Want to tell me about them.

FRANK
It's this crazy business world. You must have read about that Insurance scandle I was mixed up in?

CAVANAUGH
(nods head)
But you were cleared.

FRANK
I also lost two hundred thousand and more with that one and others. I'm just no busiiness man. If it wasn't for the paid lectures I think Floss and the kids as well as myself would starve and those four pints of blood every month just tod keep me alive... I'm in over my head and I don't know which way to turn...

CONTINUED

FL - 171.

264. CONTINUED

CAVANAUGH
How have your speeches been taken?

FRANK
Alright I guess. I get a lot of offers...

CAVANAUGH
Then I think you've answered your own problem.

FRANK
You got me there.

CAVANAUGH
If people want to hear you talk that means you have something to offer them. They want to know about you and what you've done. Write your life story.

FRANK
I'm no writer...

CAVANAUGH
Then have it done. Sell the rights to your life...it's a winner.

FRANK
You think anybody would read it John?

CAVANAUGH
They read Knute Rockne's, didn't they? And they made a hell of a movie out of his life, and your record has even surpassed his...think about it...

FRANK
I am thinking...it's a hell of an idea...Do you know somebody who might be interested?

CAVANAUGH
You can bet on it, like you always say...There's a fellow, good Irish Catholic who went right here to Notre Dame

CONTINUED

FL - 172

264. CONTINUED

CAVANAUGH (cont'd)
and he's one of your biggest fans...a guy who can really do you justice. Fellow named Bernard Williams....But come on, I'm starved, let's get to dinner. We can talk more on the way....

They prepare to leave....

FADE TO:

265. INT. LAHEY APT - PORTLAND, OREGON - BEDROOM - CLOSE PULL BACK TO MEDIUM - DAY

One grows old with time but when there is a fatal illness involved time seems to increase ten/fold. So it was with FRANK LEAHY. Seated in a chair in his bedroom he is but the shadow of his former self. When he walks he uses a cane and wibh that he is far from steady. His cheeks are shollow, his eyes sparkle, but have trouble focusing. He has been talking into the small micraphone of a tape recorder. He is chewing gum. The CAMERA PULLS BACK to take in BERNIE WILLIAMS who has been holding the tape session...a big man like most football players...(about the same age as when we saw him with his young son at the beginning.)

FRANK
...And that Bernie is where you came in to the picture...

He puts the mike down and BERNIE turns off the tape recorded.

(grin)
Took a little while, huh!!!

BERNIE
It's going to be a great book.

FRANK
Well, if anybody can tell it like it is...you're the one.

CONTINUED

FL - 173

265. CONTINUED

BERNIE
It's become more than just a story Frank...I guess you'd have to call it a labor of love with me now.

FRANK
Just do like I say and tell it as it is...Don't romance me up! I wanted to cry after I saw what they did to Knute when they did his story in the movies.

BERNIE
It's a promise...You know that.

FRANK
I don't want to let those letters out of my sight, the ones I got in the hospital those times from President Eisenhower and President Nixon, but I'll bring them when I come down to your place in Huntington Beach next week. We can have them photostated.

BERNIE
(sorrow - thinking)
Yes...that will be fine Frank.

FRANK
(catches the mood change)
Sorry Bernie. I didn't mean to remind you...you love her very much.

BERNIE
Very much...

FRANK
How is Dawna? Any better at all?

CONTINUED

FL - 174

265. CONTINUED

BERNIE
(sadly shakes
head)
Worse, if anything. The doctor's
say it's only a matter of time.

FRANK
I was given the last rites three
times with my terminal disease,
and I'm still around. Perhaps
when I come down there to see
your wife next week I can lend
a bit of moral support...after
all we are kind of birds of a
feather. What's the hospital
again?

BERNIE
Hoag Memorial in Newport Beach,
California...We'll drive down
from my place. Frank! It'll
be a great lift to her, seeing
you again.

A tear clouds FRANK'S eye and he covers it by taking the chewing gum from his mouth and tossing it into a waste basket.

FRANK
Use a lot of energy chewing gum.
I wonder just how much energy we
do use that way? Think of all
the gum chewers in the world, and
think about harnessing all that
energy...
(pace change)
I'll make it to your place if
I have to crawl.

FADE TO:

266. EXT. HOAG HOSPITAL - PARKING LOT - WIDE - DAY

BERNIE parks his car, then moves around to the passenger side and helps FRANK out. He holds the free arm while FRANK works his cane and they make their way to the entrance of the hospital.

DISSOLVE TO:

The Birth of *The Frank Leahy Legend*

This is where the screenplay starts to get meta. The first time I read it, I began to wonder just how meta it might get. Wood has Cavanaugh give Leahy the idea to write his life story, perhaps even with the aim of it becoming a movie, and even introduces Leahy to Bernie Williams.

Williams becomes a character in the action, rather than just a figure in the framing device and a narrator, in a scene set in Leahy's Portland, OR home (the Leahys actually lived in the Portland suburb Lake Oswego), where they're finishing up their series of taped interviews that form the basis of Williams' book. In Williams' book, the majority of the story is told from the point of view of Williams conducting these interviews with Leahy, but Wood has chosen to tell the tale in a more chronological manner, and has only now, in the final pages of his screenplay, caught up to where Williams' book begins.

With the mention of the goal of making a Hollywood movie based on his life story, I began to wonder if the screenplay would fill in the gaps of how Williams ended up contacting Wood to get the screenplay written. Unfortunately, Wood resists the temptation to include his part of the story, so we still don't know exactly how that transpired.

Interestingly, Wood has Leahy tell Williams he doesn't want him to romanticize his life story and only wants him to tell it like it really was. He says he hated what they did to Rockne in *Knute Rockne All American.* You only have to get a couple sentences into *The Frank Leahy Legend* to see that Williams ignored this advice – almost the entire thing is hyperbolically romantic about the greatness of Leahy. I guess from Williams' point of view, that *was* the reality of the situation.

Chewing Gum Philosophy

The first time I read this screenplay, Leahy's thoughts on chewing gum struck me as so off the wall that it must be from Wood's brain. Turns out, this chewing gum deep thought comes straight from Leahy in Williams' book. In the book, it's spoken near the beginning of the narrative. Wood saved it for near the end of the screenplay. More proof that he didn't just put his head down and do a straight page for page adaptation, but actually put thought into where he wanted things to appear in the screenplay's structure.

FL - 175

267. INT. HOSPITAL - HALL - LONG - DAY

The two men come around a corner at the end of the hall. The door they will enter is in close to the camera. Although it is not a great distance along the hall it takes the men some time to cover it. BERNIE is still holding onto FRANK'S free arm and he continually uses the cane. They pause a moment at the closed door.

BERNIE
You alright Frank?

FRANK
(hesitant)
A - little self pity,, I guess.

BERNIE opens the door and they start their entrance.

268 INT. DAWNA'S HOSPITAL ROOM - CLOSE - PULL BACK TO MEDIUM - DAY

The woman was once beautiful, but now the ravages of her disease have taken their toll (TO THE DISCRETION OF THE DIRECTOR)- The CAMERA IMMEDIATELY PULLS BACK from the sleeping tortured young woman to catch FRANK and BERNIE as they enter. They cross to the bed. The men look to each other, then BERNIE takes DAWNA'S hand.

BERNIE
Frank's here Dawna...

She does not immediately awaken. BERNIE puts a bit more pressure on her hand, and when she wakes it takes her another moment for full recognition....

DAWNA
(slowly - tortured)
Ohhh...hello darling...did you bring Frank...I so wanted to see him again.

BERNIE
Frank's here...

Painfully she turns her head so that she can look around to FRANK as he slowly comes forward, a pathetic smile...

CONTINUED

FL - 176

268. CONTINUED

It is like death greeting death.

FRANK
Hello again Dawna...

BERNIE takes his hand from hers and FRANK touches it briefly...His eyes cloud...he says no more as DAWNA'S eyes close again...

BERNIE
It's always like that...awake for a moment, then...she'll come around again.

The tears well in FRANK'S eyes and he turns to a window, grabbing at a handkerchief in his breast pocket. BERNIE goes to him.

FRANK
(slowly - tortured)
When...when I came in here I was full of self-pity...now I see her...so still...so unmoved. I can walk. I'm a bit paralized, but I can walk, get around, eat by myself...Ohhh, how can I stand this mental anguish?....

BERNIE puts his arm around his friend's shoulder.

BERNIE
I can only give you the same words, Frank, that the Pope gave us.

FRANK
(seriously - low)
The Pope?

BERNIE
When Dawna's problem first started we had an audience with Pope Paul VI - he told us "to be strong and

CONTINUED

FL - 177

268. CONTINUED

BERNIE (cont'd)
try to understand...

269. MEDIUM CLOSE - DAWNA

Her eyes flutter open. She looks toward them.

DAWNA
(light)
Why is everyone in tears?

The men walk into the scene beside her bed. She tries for a tortured smile which doesn't work. FRANK'S eyes cloud again.

(words of comfort)
I hope you overcome your difficulties, Frank....
(a continuing
XXXXXXXXXXXXXXXXXXXXXXX stab of pain racks her body)
Get...get the nurse Bernie.

BERNIE leaves the room abruptly...She writhes in pain:.FRANK stands transfixed, helplessly looking at the tortured dying woman. It is a seemingly endless moment, then BERNIE and the NURSE comes in. The two men turn away, back toward the window again as the NURSE prepares a hypo...

270. CLOSE TWO - AT THE WINDOW

BERNIE and FRANK are looking out of the window but seeing nothing.

FRANK
Strange weather for June.

BERNIE didn't answer, FRANK expected none.

FL - 178

271. WIDER

The NURSE has finished. She makes the forced grin of the official.

NURSE
She'll sleep for a few hours now...

Then she leaves the room. The men come back to the bed and look down. This time FRANK takes the girl's hand and holds it as he speaks.

FRANK
(clouded eyes)
Hang in there Damma...Hang in there.

But she is already asleep. The men make their way toward the door.

WIPE DISSOLVE

272. EXT. HOSPITAL - STEPS - MEDIUM TWO - DAY

The two men come out and FRANK pauses just outside the door. BERNIE mirrors his movements.

BERNIE
We could come back tonight...
(he knows better)

FRANK
Bernie...I...I think not.

He starts to move away, but then stops again.

You know, Bernie, one month from today I have to go back into the hospital to receive four more pints of blood. But I am contemplating acupunoture. I have heard of some marvelous results from a series of such treatments.

CONTINUED

FL - 179

272. CONTINUED

FRANK looks out over the off scene parking lot, absently, He does not look back to BERNIE as he talks.

FRANK
Bernie, I don't seem to be able to erase from my mind the vision of Dawna lying on that hospital bed. We cannot question God's plans. We cannot doubt His wisdom. But there are times when we must accept the worst, though we seem to lose our staying powers. Dawna, beautiful Dawna!
(tears)
Why? Oh, God. Why?

Then he walks off, BERNIE remains behind.

DISSOLVE TO:

273. EXT. CEMETERY - MEDIUM CLOSE - DUSK

FLOSS looks to the open grave, then after a moment she let's a flower drift into the opening. The others of the MOURNERS and FAMILy look on.

BERNIE (NAR. O.S.)
Knute Rockne had said it long ago, but the words fell equally as well to Frank Laehy. Football... It was his mother, his father and all the future relatives he would never see....

274. WIDE

As the FAMILY and MOURNERS leave the cemetery heading gack to their cars....

LONG FADE

THE END

Dawna

The crucial last few pages of this screenplay are taken up with a hospital visit to see Bernie Williams' wife, Dawna, in the hospital, where she is on her deathbed. This is true to the events of the book, and must have been very touching for both Leahy and Williams. However, it seems a strange way to spend our precious last few moments with Leahy in his life story. Narratively, it's a strange turn to take in the last few moments of the story, and distracts somewhat from Leahy's legend. Thematically, Wood is attempting to tie it into Leahy's looming death, which Williams does as well, in the book, but it doesn't quite come off.

Two Endings

Wood provides two endings here, one labeled "ALTERNATE END" in handwriting. The first features Floss at Leahy's grave, which is in Mt. Calvary Catholic Cemetery, Portland, OR. The second features an old and frail Leahy walking through the hospital parking lot when a dissolve replaces the parking lot with the Notre Dame football field and elderly Leahy with his younger athletic self, walking the empty football field alone. This is somewhat reminiscent of the ending of *Knute Rockne All American,* featuring a transparent ghostly vision of Rockne walking the football field alone, and makes me wonder if that's what Wood had in mind.

It would be interesting to know the origin of the idea to include two endings. Either Wood was uncertain how to end the screenplay so just decided to provide variety, or Williams potentially requested a couple options for the end. If I had to choose, I think I'd choose the alternate ending – the last few pages have already been bleak and have strayed from Leahy's legend a bit, so it's nice to end on a reminder of why we're watching a movie about Leahy in the first place – his successes at Notre Dame.

"THE FRANK LEAHY LEGEND"

CAST IN ORDER OF APPEARANCE

CAST	BITS	EXTRAS
BERNIE	YOUNG BERNIE	MR. PAUGH
FRANK LEAHY SR.	YOUNG GENE	FARM PEOPLE (fire)
MRS. LEAHY	YOUNG MARIE	TIME-KEEPER (fight)
FRANK	MIDWIFE	DANCE HALL PEOPLE
GENE	YOUNG FRANK	PAPER BOY
KNUTE ROCKNE	TEEN GENE	PEOPLE (Speak-Easy)
TOMMY MILLS	TEEN MARIE	PLAYERS (horse bit)
MOON MULLINS	YOUNG ANN	
JOHN CAVANAUGH	YOUNG EILEEN	
TEAM DOCTOR	TEEN FRANK	
	HIGH SCHOOL COACH(WALSH)	
	SILENT JOE BALAH	
	JOE'S MANAGER	
	REFEREE (fight)	
	SPECTATOR (fight)	
	DRUNK (fight)	
	THIN MAN (Dance Hall)	
	PRETTY GIRL (Dance Hall)	
	DRUNK (Dance Hall)	
	CLAYTON	
	BLONDE	
	BRUNETTE	
	YOUNG TOM	
	MILLER	

CAST IN ORDER OF APPEARANCE - Page 2 - ("THE FRANK LEAHY LEGEND")

CAST	BITS	EXTRAS
	1st STUDENT (Hall seq)	STUDENTS (Fr. Class)
	2nd STUDENT (Hall sez)	STUDENT (X-Mas)
	FATHER O'DELL (Hall seq)	WASHT. HALL BOYS
	FATHER MICHEL (French)	QUARY WORKMEN
	STEVE (Rm. Mate)	SMALL TOWN PEOPLE
	QUARRY FOREMAN	SMALL TOWN BASE.PLRS.
	HENRY	SPEECH CLASS
	YOUNG MAN (1st theatre)	MOVIE THEATRE PEOPLE
	FATHER DONELLY (Speech)	MOVIE COMPANY
	MOVIE DIRECTOR	O.S. CAMERMAN
	PRIEST (Movie seq)	XXXXXXXXXXXXXXXXXX
	JEFF (Railroad car)	BON FIRE PEOPLE
	CHURCH PRIEST	SPEAK-PEOPLE (Leahy)
	JERRY	PRIEST (Funeral Leah
	TERRI (Follies girl)	MOURNERS (Fune.Leahy
	ASST. COACH (Elbow bit)	SPECTATORS (game)
	XXXXXX ANNOUNCER	MICHIGAN PLAYERS
	BARTENDER (Leach bit)	FORDHAM PLAYERS
	1st HEAVY	
	2nd HEAVY	
	NURSE	
	SLEEPY JOE CRAWLEY	
	XXXXXXXX CARBERRY	
	TOM DWYER	

CAST IN ORDER OF APPERANCE - Page 3 -("THE FRANK LEAHY LEGEND)

CAST	BITS	EXTRAS
FLORENCE (FLOSS) REILLY	ANN MC CAFFERTY	BOSTON U. PLAYERS
ZIGGY CZAROBSKI	YOUNG FELLOW (Movies)	TRAIN PLAT. PEOPLE
MOOSE KRAUSE	JOE (Bussinessman)	MAN (War)
JOHNNY LATTNER	JACK CURLEY	NOTRE DAME PLAYERS (note, must be changed often as the years and the Tech. Director Designates)
JOHNNY LUJAK	2nd ANNOUNCER	
ORACKO	LELLIS	
FATHER HESBURGH	MR. CZAROBSKI	
	BARTENDER (War)	PRIESTS (Hesburgh seq)
	REFEREE (Dog Seq.)	
	FRANK II (Young)	
	SUSAN (young)	
	LIVINGSTON	
	KEAGAN	
	LIMONT	
	WHITE	
	(2nd) MILLER	
	DOCTOR (Hospital)	
	SCOREKEEPER (Oracko bit)	
	1st DRUNK (Oracko bit)	
	2nd DRUNK (Oracko bit)	
	CINDY (Firehouse bit)	
	1st PRIEST (Firehouse seq)	
	2nd PRIEST (Firehouse seq)	
	ELDERLY JANITOR (PATRICK)	
	OFFICE DOCTOR	

CAST IN ORDER OF APPEARANCE - Page 4 - (THE FRANK LEAHY LEGEND)

CAST	BITS	EXTRAS
LOU WOLFSON	SECRETARY (Wolfson seq)	WOLFSON MEN
	DAWNA	
	NURSE (Dawna seq)	

" THE FRANK LEAHY LEGEND"

INTERRIOR SET LIST

FOOTBALL HALL OF FAME - DAY

LEAHY FARM - LIVING ROOM - NEBRASKA - NIGHT

LEAHY FARM - BEDROOM - NEBRASKA - NIGHT

INT. LEAHY BARN - WINNER, SOUTH DAKOTA - DAY

INT. LEAHY KITCHEN - WINNER, SOUTH DAKOTA - DAY & NIGHT

HIGH SCHOOL BASKETBALL COURT - WINNER - DAY

FRANK & GENE'S BEDROOM - WINNER - NIGHT

INT. BOXING BARN - NIGHT

DANCE HALL - WINNER - NIGHT

HIGH SCHOOL SHOWER @ WINNER - DAY

SPEAK-EASY - WINNER - NIGHT

RECREATION ROOM - NOTRE DAME - NIGHT & DAY

LONG HALLWAY - DORMITORY - NIGHT - NOTRE DAME

FRENCH CLASSROOM - DAY - NOTRE DAME

FRANK'S ROOM - DORMITORY - NIGHT - NOTRE DAME

UNIVERSITY KITCHEN - NOTRE DAME- NIGHT

WASHINGTON HALL - HALL - NOTRE DAME - NIGHT

1st MOVIE THEATER - NIGHT

SPEECH CLASS - NOTRE DAME - DAY

RAILROAD DINING CAR - LATE DAY

KNUTE ROCKNE'S OFFICE - DAY - NOTRE DAME

INT. CHURCH - NOTRE DAME - DAY

1st LOCKER ROOM - GAME - DAY

PRESS ROOM - DAY

" THE FRANK LEAHY LEGEND " - INTERRIOR SET LIST - Page 2

TERRI'S APARTMENT - NIGHT

TUNNEL TO FIELD - DAY

2nd LOCKER ROOM - DAY

1st HOSPITAL ROOM - DAY

RUSTIC SPEAK-EASY (WINNER ?) - NIGHT

3rd LOCKER ROOM - DAY

4th LOCKER ROOM - DAY

2nd HOSPITAL ROOM

PROJECTION ROOM - NOTRE DAME - D/N

LECTURE ROOM - NIGHT

FRANK'S ROOM - FORDHAM - NIGHT

FLOSS' HOME - HALL - NIGHT

FLOSS' HOME - LIVING ROOM - NIGHT

2nd MOVIE THEATRE - NIGHT - (MAIN SCENE as well as MONTAGE seq)

SODA FOUNTAIN - NIGHT (for MONTAGE SEQ.)

2nd BASKETBALL COURT - DAY

LEAHY LIVING ROOM - FORDHAM - NIGHT

leahy living room - BOSTON - DAY

announcers booth - BOSTON - DAY/N

LEAHY'S OFFICE (FIREHOUSE ?) - NOTRE DAME - DAY & NIGHT

MEAT MARKET - DAY

LEAHY LIVING ROOM - SOUTH BEND - NIGHT

RESTAURANT - DAY

CAVANAUGH'S OFFICE - DAY - NOTRE DAME

LEAHY BASEMENT - SOUTH BEND - DAY

3rd HOSPITAL ROOM - NIGHT

"THE FRANK LEAHY LEGEND" - INTERRIOR SET LIST - Page 3

INT. 5th LOCKER ROOM - DAY

BOARD ROOM - NOTRE DAME - DAY

T.V. STATION (for T.V. reception)

6th LOCKER ROOM - DAY

HALLWAY - TO LOCKER ROOM # 6 - DAY

4th HOSPITAL ROOM - DAY

DOCTOR'S OFFICE

AUDITORIUM - NOTRE DAME - DAY

FOYER - WOLFSON OFFICE - DAY

BOARD ROOM - WOLFSON OFFICE - DAY

COURT ROOM - DAY

LEAHY BEDROOM - PORTLAND, OREGON - DAY

CORRIDOR - HOAG HOSPITAL - DAY

DAWNA'S HOSPITAL ROOM - DAY

"THE FRANK LEAHY LEGEND"

EXTERIOR SET LIST

FOOTBALL HALL OF FAME - NOTRE DAME - DAY

leahy farm - NEBRASKA - NIGHT

LEAHY HOUSE - WINNER, SOUTH DAKOTA - DAY

LEAHY BARN - WINNER, SOUTH DAKOTA - DAY

(for montage seq) SHOVELING SNOW - DELIVERING PAPERSPICKING FRUIT, SWEEPING SIDEWALKS IN FRONT OF STORES, etc.) 2nd Unit.

DANCE HALL - WINNER - NIGHT

NOTRE DAME UNIVERSITY - ESTABLISHING - DAY

NOTRE DAME PRACTICE FIELD - ESTABLISHING - DAY

DORMITORY - NOTRE DAME - NIGHT

GOLDEN DOME - NOTRE DAME - NIGHT

WASHINGTON HALL - NOTRE DAME - NIGHT

ROCK QUARRY - DAY

BASEBALL FIELD - DAY

CHURCH - NOTRE DAME - DAY

RALLEY FOR (NOTRE DAME vs ?) - NIGHT

SPEAK EASY - (WINNER ???) - NIGHT

DIRT ROAD - (WINNER ????) - NIGHT

CEMETERY # 1 - (WINNER ????) - DAY

GAME # 1 - DAY

PRACTICE FIELD - GEORGTOWN UNIVERSITY - DAY

practice field - MICHIGAN STATE - DAY

GAME # 2 - FORDHAM - DAY

(for MONTAGE SEQ. - Movie THEATRE - AMUSEMENT PARK RIDING IN OPEN CAR, etc.) WITH FLOSS bit.

"THE FRANK LEAHY LEGEND" - EXTERIOR SET LIST - Page 2

PRACTICE FIELD - FORDHAM - DAY

20th CENTURY LIMITED - PLATFORM - DAY

GAME # 3 - DAY

NOTRE DAME STADIUM - DAY

GAME # 4 - NOTRE DAME & ARMY - DAY

BLEECHERS - NOTRE DAME & ARMY - DAY

CEMETERY # 2

GAME # 5 - WITH HEADLINES SHOOTING IN

GAME # 6 - Oracko bit - DAY

FIRE HOUSE OFFICE - NIGHT

GAME # 6 - NOTRE DAME vs GEORGIA TECH. - DAY

GAME # 7 - MONTAGE OF SCENES - DAY

EXT. HOAG HOSPITAL - PARKING LOT - DAY

CEMETERY # #3

Afterword: Leahy… Post Mortem

by W. Paul Apel

The other day, on the trail of Ed Wood, I found myself in a real "Bob and Shirley" type situation. You know them – the lead couple in Wood's *Orgy of the Dead.* Like them, I was driving down a winding road looking for a cemetery. Don't worry, I didn't get into a wreck and I didn't run afoul of the Emperor of the Dead and his bevy of beautiful dancing ghouls. I did get lost, though. Sort of.

It was a fairly typical Pacific Northwest day, only without the rain – sometimes the clouds rolled in and it was gloomy, other times they rolled away and it was sun and blue skies. I was searching for the Mt. Calvary Cemetery, within the city limits of Portland, OR but way up in the evergreen tree-lined West Hills, on a stretch of Burnside I'd never had reason to travel before.

What does Ed Wood have to do with the second oldest Catholic cemetery in Multnomah County? Simple: the trail of Ed Wood has crossed with the trail of famed Notre Dame coach, Frank Leahy, who lived out the last years of his life in and around Portland, OR and was laid to rest at Mt. Calvary in 1973 after a long battle with leukemia and heart disease. Not many years later his wife, Florence (everyone called her "Floss"), joined him.

I had finally gotten my hands on Wood's screenplay, *The Frank Leahy Legend,* and given it most likely one of its first reads in 40-some years, surprised to find a scene near the end set in Portland, OR. Having lived here for most of my adult life and grown up in a small town outside the city, it was fun to know that the events of Leahy's life had required Wood's fingers to type those words so often typed by me – Portland, OR.

It took me a couple weeks to internalize this to the point where I realized that if Leahy died in Portland, he was likely buried there, too. Which meant I could go visit his grave. Which is how I ended up making like Bob and Shirley one spring afternoon.

I always underestimate cemeteries. They're always bigger than I think they'll be, and everything is harder to find than I think it'll be.

I made sure to look up Leahy's final resting place online before setting out, and even tried to use a handy online map Mt. Calvary has on their website while I was at the cemetery, to try to orient myself. And I still got lost.

The first thing I did was blow right by the cemetery's main entrance. So, I turned into the next entrance I could find and found myself winding through hills of beautiful green grass, surrounded on all sides by headstones. The thing about cemetery roads is that they're always just a little too small to seem passable by two cars at once and never make it clear whether they're one way or both ways or what. Every time I've ever tried to navigate a cemetery, I have always worried I'm going to ruin some mourner's day by inadvertently blocking their path. Under normal circumstances if you get stuck on a small road, you can just turn around. In a cemetery, one false move and you risk desecration.

I figured the best thing for it was to navigate myself through the cemetery until I got to the main entrance, park, re-orient myself from there and hoof it. That's what I did, but as soon as I got to the top of my first hill, I realized this place was way too big for hoofing, especially if I was lost. Like the patrolman said in *Plan 9 from Outer Space*, "It's hard to find something when you don't know what you're looking for."

What would Bob and Shirley do? Well, Bob would be useless and Shirley would scream. I didn't want to scream and I was already useless, so I got back in the car and thought maybe if I drove slowly enough I could figure it out. As I went, I located small markers that said which part of the cemetery I was in – hard to read from the car, but possible. I was looking for W, and after a while, found it. I parked and walked around a bit, up and down the paved road, looking at the vast swath of grass and graves that made up W, thinking how it'd be way too hard to go out there and walk back and forth looking for a headstone. The app I was using was trying to tell me specifically where I could find the stone, but I couldn't make heads or tails of it. Like Glen in *Glen or Glenda*, my mind was in a muddle.

On top of that, the clock was ticking. Don't tell my boss but between you and me, I ran out during lunch thinking I could find Leahy's grave and come back before anyone missed me. Time was running out and I still had nothing to show for the search. I went back to the car and moved it a couple times, up the hill, down the hill, got out, walked around, stared at the app.

Then, a miracle occurred. I don't know how, but suddenly, just as I was about to give up, I took one last look at the map on my phone, and everything seemed to lock into place. It was as if Leahy himself had looked down from above and made a command by quoting his favorite poem: "Don't quit." The going was tough, so I got going, and within a couple minutes there I stood – looking down at Leahy's modest marker.

I knelt down and brushed the freshly mown grass away from it. Then, I took the paper out that I had brought with me and set it on the stone. The cover page of *The Frank Leahy Legend*, by Edward D. Wood, Jr., complete with Ed's own handwritten initials. At last, and probably for the first time, Leahy had been united with the screenplay of his life.

Eddie, meet Frank, I thought. *Frank, meet Eddie.*

I took a look around. It was not a bad view and it was a beautiful day. Birds chirped. The hum of groundskeepers keeping the grounds floated by. An elderly mourner in the distance got back in his car, his visit with his loved one finished for the day. I took my cue from him. Time to return to the land of the living. After all, I was late for work.

About the Author

W. Paul Apel grew up in McMinnville, OR and received his B.A. in Creative Writing from the University of Redlands in Redlands, CA. He has worked as a cartoonist, landscaping assistant, movie theater usher, film critic, video store clerk, golf course groundskeeper, barista, writing tutor and account representative. He currently writes ad copy in Portland, OR. This is his first book.

www.ingramcontent.com/pod-product-compliance
Ingram Content Group UK Ltd.
Pitfield, Milton Keynes, MK11 3LW, UK
UKHW021712190726
13853UKWH00001B/498

9 798887 712116